Viewing Boxing From Ringside

Viewing Boxing From Ringside

Frank Lotierzo
Tom Donelson

Writers Club Press
San Jose New York Lincoln Shanghai

Viewing Boxing From Ringside

Writers Club Press
an imprint of iUniverse, Inc.

For information address:
iUniverse, Inc.
5220 S. 16th St., Suite 200
Lincoln, NE 68512
www.iuniverse.com

ISBN: 0-595-23748-7

Printed in the United States of America

Tom's Dedication

This book is dedicated to my many friends old and new.

To Annie, Scott, Peggy, Kim and Carol, your words of advice and encouragement were always appreciated.

To my wife, Janice and two children, Bethany and Kat, thanks for your patience.

To Frank, you are the best collaborator any man can have.

To my Parents, you are the greatest.

Tom
6-23-02

Frank's Dedication

To My friend Tom,

Thanks so much for taking me along with you on this project. You are the sole reason for this. Without your insight and dedication, it wouldn't have gotten off the ground. Yes, it has been a labor of Love for both of us and a ton of fun, but it took your planning and foresight. Boxing is a passion that we both share and I'm honored that you asked me to be a part of it. You are a terrific writer and an even better person. Thanks again and all the best to you and yours.

Your friend,

Frank
6-23-02

Contents

Acknowledgments

Frank and I would like to acknowledge the following people for their help in writing this book. First of all, we wish to acknowledge the staff members of Cyberboxingzone.com, especially Steve Gordan, J.D. Vena and Tracy Callis for their insight and excellent historical perspective.

We also wish to thank Kim Smith and Carol Golden for their help in editing and reviewing the manuscript as well as graphic design. Their long hours, working for less than minimum wage, was important to the final product that is before you. We also like to thank other friends such as Richard Reynolds, Peg Antonelli, Annie Wilcox and her husband Scott for their advice and words of encouragements.

And finally, we thank our wives, Janice and Terri and in Tom's case, his children for tolerating the time it took to write this book.

Preface

My own athletic career includes running track and cross-country in college, then running for a couple of track clubs for nearly a decade after college. At the age of 31, I started in martial arts—eventually earning a black belt. Along the way, I had the chance to train with professional kickboxers and it was there I learned the sacrifice and skills needed to be successful at the highest levels. Boxing, as sport, has always fascinated me. In this sport two men go in the ring, one man leaving victorious.

Frank Lotierzo has been around boxing rings all his life. After a successful amateur career and an undefeated boxing career cut short by injuries, Frank Lotierzo maintained his interest in boxing including writing about it. Frank is a sharp observer of boxing and I have learned a lot about the sweet science from my exchanges with Frank and with other members of **Cyberboxingzone.com**.

The idea for this book came from exchanges with Frank and I over pieces we both published in Cyberboxingzone.com. We decided after these exchanges to write a book, featuring our previous pieces that we had published with new pieces added. We wanted a book that would give the reader observations about boxing, adding stories about some of the most notable characters of the sport. In addition, we had the chance to communicate with several boxing experts about ideas contained in this book. These contacts led to several exchanges, and in the end, added to the book. I found myself learning more about the sport and many preconceived notions that I did have, simply disappeared. Other opinions have been strengthened, after being exposed to new facts and new thoughts. We have included in this book interviews with many of these experts that impacted our own thoughts.

This book will introduce you to boxers that you may not have heard of, but whose stories need to be told. Boxers like Harry Wills, an African-American fighter denied a chance to fight for the Heavyweight crown during the 1920's. We also challenged and rethought great controversies. For example, we examined the career of Jack Dempsey and his most noble rival, Gene Tunney with our conclusion sure to cause debates.

Read this book and be prepared to be challenged. If you finish this book with a better appreciation of the sport and better understanding of major characters such as Muhammad Ali, Joe Louis, Jack Dempsey, Gene Tunney, Floyd Patterson as well as modern day warriors including Lennox Lewis and Evander Holyfield-then, we have succeeded.

Tom Donelson
June 22, 2002

Foreword

By Dan Cuoco
Director, International Boxing Research Organization (IBRO)

It's a curious thing about boxing fans. They seem more enthralled about hypothetical pairings than in anything else. And I must admit I'm no different. And the beauty about hypothetical theories is that everyone has an opinion as to why their opinions are correct. You can believe what you want, and people can argue until they're too hoarse to talk, in the final analysis you can't prove a thing.

The biggest arguments lately seem to settle in on the heavyweight division. After all, the magnetism of the heavyweight championship (and I'm talking linear, not the phony alphabet titles) is unequalled, in my humble opinion, as a world sporting attraction even today. Even the English were torn between watching England's participation in the World Cup and the Lewis-Tyson fight. The reason—what other sporting event remains so unique for pre-event furore, fills you with the tension of the moment and for sustained post-event comment.

For your reading pleasure Tom Donelson and Frank Lotierzo have put together a series of their boxing essays on such legendary performers as Muhammad Ali, Joe Louis, Jack Dempsey, Gene Tunney, Floyd Patterson, Sugar Ray Robinson and many more from the past as well as modern day warriors such as Lennox Lewis, Evander Holyfield and Mike Tyson.

Their essays do not attempt to span boxing's rich history; they merely are intended to provide a picture of a variety of fighters and to judge them on the basis of their distinctive qualities.

To that end, I think Tom and Frank do an excellent job of portraying the essence of the sport of boxing through the quality of their observations about boxing and the short bios about some of the most notable characters of the sport.

This book is not only an enjoyable read, but will also stimulate further dialogue among boxing fans.

Foreword: A View From A Fan

By Carol Golden

I now see Boxing history through a whole new lens. Boxing legends came alive before my eyes and I understood finally what brought them to the levels they attained. Listening to my parents talk about Joe Louis and remembering Cassius Clay/Ali from my own early adult years enhanced the information gleaned from these pages.

New names were dangled before me and now I want to know more about them. Where was I when they fought for glory? What kind of lives did they lead? Now I am on a treasure hunt for answers to those questions. This book has whet my appetite for more.

Carol Golden-Media Assistant, Marion, IA

Boxing, Why We Love It

By Tom Donelson
Published in July's Cyberboxingzone.com

The famous sports writer Red Smith described boxing as the red light district of sports. In spite of the whores, con artists and all around wise guys that populate the boxing scene, boxing still remains enthralling. My love affair with boxing began as a kid in the 60's, following Ali's career. It was Ali's mastery of the ring that enticed me into boxing and his grace and nobility in the ring that grabbed my interest.

Obviously boxing was more than just Ali, and historically, the heavyweight champion was the most famous sports figure in America. During the roaring 20's, Jack Dempsey's earnings dwarfed that of even Babe Ruth and this despite fighting just four of the seven years that he was Heavyweight champion. A reporter once asked Babe Ruth why he was earning more money than President Herbert Hoover. Ruth replied, "I had a better year than the President." (In Ruth's defense, he did have a better year than Hoover, who managed America into the great depression.) Dempsey's earnings not only dwarfed the great Babe, but his earnings dwarfed those of all the Presidents throughout the 20's.

Boxing as a sport never advanced beyond its medieval past of the early part of the previous century. It should be noted that sports in the early 20th century fell victim to crooks and con artists. Corruption affected Baseball, the American pastime, at the turn of the 20th century. The "Black Sox" Scandal demonstrated that even the World Series was not exempt from the criminal element, as members of the White Sox threw the 1919 World Series. The difference was that Baseball decided to put its house in order and ensure that this would not happen again. It began with a central authority resting in the hands of Judge Landis, who banned every member of the White Sox involved in throwing the World Series from the game forever. Baseball began the process of protecting its integrity and enjoyed massive popularity as America's pastime until Football took over in the 1960's. Most sports followed baseball's lead in establishing a central authority to protect their integrity. Boxing did not. Promoters have always treated boxing as a fiefdom and no central authority has ever existed to promote the sport. The sport survived in spite of itself. In the 20's, the Mafia began the process of controlling the sport and this continued until the early 60's. Now major promoters such as Don King and Bob Arum rule the sport through various sanctioning bodies, which do their bidding.

This has hurt boxing in the past twenty years. Since Ali left the boxing scene and Mike Tyson self-destructed, boxing has done everything it could to commit suicide. Boxing survives, but boxing today no longer has the same hold upon the sporting imagination. Most fights are on cable or pay for view. If ESPN, HBO and Showtime did not cover the sport, no one would.

So why does boxing still survive? It is the nature of humans to pummel one another and boxing is merely the reminder of man's early struggle. War is the one reality of humankind, and boxing is a reflection of man's violent nature. Only there are rules within the ring. It is the one place where natural aggressiveness is allowed and cheered. Men will fight for 36 minutes, looking for their moment of glory—a shot at a championship belt. When it is over, most fighters merely congratulate each other. For combat only exists within the ring, and after the bell rings the final time man's violent nature gives way to his sporting instinct. Boxers more than any other athletes understand the sacrifice needed to fight and they are most respectful of their opponents. The hatred that exists within the confines of the boxing ring disappears after it is over. Boxers understand that their opponents have traveled the same path. Bravado exists in all boxers but there is humility as well.

Boxers understand that defeat can happen in the next fight and there is no place for arrogance for even the greatest will fall prey to age. The greatest fighters found themselves victims of their own hubris as they fought just one more fight. They only deluded themselves in thinking that they could be the fighters who beat the ravages of age. No one beats the aging process and in the end, even the greatest must face defeat, humiliation, and retirement.

Ali as a young man bragged about being the greatest, but near the end of his career, he began to see his own mortality. After the Thrilla in Manila, Ali tried to heal the rift with his most noble opponent, Smokin' Joe Frazier. Ali learned to respect the man he taunted for nearly 5 years and whom he fought 41 of the toughest rounds in Heavyweight history. Humility came as the result of punches that landed upon Ali's body and head. After the Thrilla in Manila, Ali became more humble and appreciative of the sport that he mastered. When Holmes fought Ali, it would be Holmes toughest moment. Forced to fight an aging Ali, whose eroding skills merely made Ali a target, Holmes beat the defenseless ex-champion. Holmes saw his own future boxing demise, losing to Mike Tyson eight years later as an aging former champion. Every fighter must face defeat and face it alone. A football player is but one of eleven players and a basketball player is but one of five players. Even in defeat, a basketball or football player will never truly be signaled out for he is part of a team. A boxer faces his opponent alone and there is no one else who can help. Hit or be hit, that is the fate of a boxer. Boxing is the noble sport, incapable of being destroyed by the many princes who rule the sport as their own fiefdom. Boxing has survived because boxing is bigger than the rulers of the sport and it survives because we see human frailty and courage on display in every bout. Boxing is the last place for the modern day warrior outside of war. As Joyce Carol Oates observed, "Boxing is for men, and is about men, and is men. A celebration of the lost art of masculinity all the more trenchant for being lost."

Finally, Boxing is a sport at its most brutal, most primitive, and most natural. Two men defending their honor and courage, in a ring surrounded by observers, whose love for the sport is essentially spiritual. Boxing is the last refuge of the modern day warrior.

Forever Noble

by Tom Donelson
(First published in March, Wail Cyberboxingzone.com)

The great fighters know no pain, no understanding of defeat, for they are the modern day gladiators, willing to die before defeat. No amount of punishment will stop them, eyes closed, ribs broken, arms bruised and yet they keep fighting. The fighter feels the scar of every punch that lands, and yet he blocks out all the pain for that one chance at the championship belt. Boxing reporter Mark Kram even suspected this sadistic behavior may have a sexual overtone for some fighters, when he wrote, "I suspected that the best fighters are sadomasochists who abjure pain in their words while secretly warm to it. Old trainers used to tell me that they had known fighters who got hit so much that it became pleasurable, they even ejaculated…but the history of orgasm pursuit.. suggesting that no stone has ever been unturned." In a boxer's career, there is no part of his body that does not take a horrific beating. Paul Simon's song, "the Boxer", details the plight of the prizefighter as he remembers every punch delivered, every cut that scars his face. Chuck Wepner has a boxer's face, with scar tissue making up most of what was once a human face.

Wepner, who became the influence for the Rocky's series starring Sylvester Stallone, often used his face to block punches. His fight with Ali was a lesson in survival as he caught Ali's punches one after another. In another fight against Sonny Liston, Wepner needed so many stitches after soaking up Liston's sledgehammer shots, that Liston commented wryly that Wepner's manager was even braver than Wepner, in allowing Wepner to continue to fight.

Randall "Tex" Cobb took the sadomasochist side of boxing to yet another level when he confronted Larry Holmes for a championship fight. Cobb, who never was a big puncher, stood in the middle of the ring and took whatever Larry Holmes delivered. By the ninth round, Cobb's face was a bloody mess but his corner showed no inclination to stop the fight. Howard Cosell yelled for the fight to be stopped from his ringside broadcast booth as there was nothing left to be gained by continuing the fight. Cobb did not quit and had no intentions of quitting. For Cobb, winning ceased to be a goal but survival was. To be able to say, I stood toe to toe with Larry Holmes, was enough. For some boxers, victory is not the goal, but fighting is. It is what they do and what they enjoy. The cuts sustained in a fight are nothing more than a bloody red badge of courage to be savored. For Cobb and Wepner, every punch delivered is etched on their face and their looks are the final mark of their trade. Cauliflower ears and flattened nose, with nothing but cartilage left is the final reminder of a boxer's life.

In boxing, cowardice is exposed and bravery is exalted. For a boxer to quit on his stool is the worst cruelty of all. When Sonny Liston sat on his stool and refused to come out to fight Ali in the seventh round of their first fight, his career was over. A reputation built on raw power and intimidation ceased to exist and the word "quitter" was attached to his image, forever. It is said that a coward dies a thousand deaths and Sonny Liston's own reputation is forever sullied by his failure to answer the bell against Ali. That is a fate worse than death.

In the Thrilla in Manila, Ali and Frazier showed boxing at its most brutal and noble, simultaneously. Ali was the favorite and no one really expected this fight to go the distance. For the first four rounds, Ali was determined to end the fight early as he kept hitting Frazier with accurate combinations. Frazier kept coming forward, taking the punishment and featuring a punishing body attack as fierce as ever seen in the heavyweight division, Frazier turned the tide, beginning in the fifth round. During these middle rounds, Ali mockingly asked, "They said you were through, Frazier" and Frazier replied, "They lied, Pretty boy." This fight was not about the championship but about who was the better fighter, Frazier or Ali. For both men, death was preferable to defeat.

After many years of verbal abuse at the hands of Ali, Frazier was ready for his payback. Ali was ready to quit at the end of the 10th round after telling his corner; this was the "closest to dying he ever experienced." In every fighter's career, there is a time in which the fighter's energy is depleted and nothing is left in the proverbial gas tank. The fighter must struggle to find one more ounce of reserve. Ali found that reserve against his most determined foe yet. Over the next four rounds, the tide turned once again in Ali's favor. In the 13th round, Ali sent Frazier's mouthpiece flying into the seventh row, and in the 14th round, Ali threw one right hand after another, Frazier powerless to stop him. Eyes closed, Frazier could no longer see and was no longer able to defend himself. All he had left was will and the willingness to die in the ring. Both Ali and Frazier showed nobility in the ring. As Eddie Futch whispered into Frazier's ear before stopping the fight, "You will be remembered for what you did today." In the "Thrilla in Manila", Ali and Frazier were ennobled by their performance and the fight became part of boxing folklore.

A fighter is in the end, judged by the pain he tolerates as opposed to the fights he wins. Boxing fans dismiss victory without pain and suffering. For suffering and the tolerance of pain defines the fighter. Nothing solidified a boxer more in the eyes of his fans than the pain tolerated in the pursuit of his craft. Pain, brutality and courage are what give prizefighters their notoriety and fame.

May 30, 2001
Ghosts of Manila

By Mark Kram
First published in KC Jones June 2001 and Wail October 2001,
Cyberboxingzone.com
By Tom Donelson

o o o o o o o o o o o o o o o o o o o o o o o o o o o o

"Fighters know how to suffer. They demagnify pain and seldom talk about it. Though some fighters have been called "bow-wows" within the sport, thresholds of pain are hard to detect in fighters.... Eyes, nose, ears, larynx, kidneys, they all take horrific beatings. But their faces tell where fighters have been, the potholes over which they had to rattle, from the small arenas with the single light bulb and a backed-up toilet in the dressing rooms to the floodlights of the big time"

——Mark Kram

Mark Kram has produced the politically incorrect but more accurate picture of the Ali-Frazier rivalry that not only shaped a sport but a society as well. There was a time in which Heavyweight champions were as famous as Presidents and no one was bigger than Ali. Ali matched superior boxing skills with a PR machine that has not been seen before or since in the boxing universe. Even today, Ali is treated more as a Greek God than a popular sporting figure. For many, he has become a symbol of the rebellious 60's.

Boxing heroes are usually defined less by the ease of their victories than by their defeats and their various comebacks in the course of a career. Fighters are made through the brutal confines of their sport, in which they nearly see death approach, where their blood is splattered and yet they somehow perservere. Brutality sells tickets but more importantly, it seals one's fame. For Ali, Joe Frazier was his ticket to fame.

There were two Ali careers. Before being forced into boxing exile after refusing induction into the armed forces, Ali easily dominated the heavyweight scene with ease. Rarely did he have to work up a sweat and his athletic skills dominated the universe he fought in. Even though he outsized most heavyweights, his hand and foot speed was that of a welterweight. His athletic skills allowed him to break all of boxing's rules and, as Mark Kram observed, he rarely listened to his corner man, Angelo Dundee, one of boxing's greatest. He marched to his own beat, never really learning basic boxing tenets only because his speed allowed him to break all rules.

The Ali that came back from exile was a little slower and, suddenly, he was faced with fighters, who would have been great in any other era. George Foreman, who would win the heavyweight title a second time at the age of 45, was one of the most feared sluggers of his era. Ali merely made him look silly. But it was Joe Frazier, a fighter whose own greatness was overshadowed by Ali, who pushed Ali to his limits of endurance.

Joe Frazier, like Foreman, would have dominated in most eras of boxing. He was the Mike Tyson of his era, a man whose left hook crushed anything human it came in contact with. He was a perpetual machine, always moving, always punching, never stopping. He was the foil that made Ali great.

Mark Kram demystifies several myths about Ali. He leaves no doubt that the Black Muslims of the mid 60's were of violent bent . Ali was their tool, their PR machine that they used to their advantage. It was Mark Kram's contention that the Muslims engineered Ali's opposition to the Vietnam War and later, his refusal to join the army. Sugar Ray

Robinson, the great middleweight and one of Ali's mentors, always suspected that Ali feared his own Muslim friends and his stand on the military may have reflected his relationship with the Black Muslims. The late Malcolm X warned Ali when he joined the Black Muslims, "Nobody leaves the Muslims without trouble." Kram's own impression of Ali's early relationship with the Muslims was that Ali "had no import in Muslim decision-making; he was a useful idiot with a name to them."

Ali's myth making was a product of the media then and now. Mark Kram writes, "The press coverage of Ali (seldom called by that name) and his troubles was as misguided and excessive as the throwing of flowers in his path today." Much of his negative press had less to do with racism than to a divide that existed between traditional liberals, who were veterans of World War II and Korea, and the hard left that dominates the media today. Many of Ali's media opposition were card-carrying members of the Democrat Party of that era. Kram noted that reporters "didn't prattle absolute role models. Hardly saints themselves, their private sins were ignored. If they had a central complaint against Clay, it was that they believed him to be a phony and sin of all sins, unheroic." There were media leaders who sided with Ali as well.

Howard Cosell made his fame and reputation on Ali but as Mark Kram reports, Cosell did not initially risk his media career to side with Ali, coming aboard when it became apparent that it could be a career maker. Kram was no fan of Cosell and found Cosell's relationship with Ali as more self-serving than heroic. Kram considers Cosell, "a horn poseur, a formerly dismissable amoeba in the lawyer chain who found TV, and one day would think he was worthy of being a senator. Those who came after him would imitate and amplify his cheap theatrics, then liken him to the Edward R. Murrow of sports. He became the pioneer for their license to break through their puffed hair and crayon content and be real journalists. A model who, with faux outrage and oily uninformed syntax, could not lay the slightest claim to even the more base rudiments of the craft."

He is even more harsh of a young Bryant Gumbel, who as the editor of Black Sports not only worshipped the ground Ali walked on, but was always willing to strip more flesh off his most notable rival, Joe Frazier. Kram's opinion of Gumbel was not very high to say the least, as he accused Mr. Gumbel of being a "mediocre writer and thinker, excellent qualifications for the large success he would have on television's Today Show, with a shallow hard-worked ultra-sophistication, a cool broker of opinion next to Howard Cosell's weaselly conniving."

Gumbel is representative of Ali supporters then and now. He, like others, is responsible for covering up Ali's own cruelty to selective opponents. Gumbel authored a piece after Frazier's victory over Ali in the first part of their trilogy, "Is Joe Frazier a White Champion in Black Skin?" One of most interesting ironies of Ali's career is that he dissed his black opponents far more than his white opponents. He tortured and taunted Floyd Patterson in their first fight and literally beat the life out of Ernie Terrill in their match in 1966. In Ali's defense, these opponents were dismissive of his conversion to the Black Muslims, and his battles against them were as much a holy war as a boxing match. But his worst treatment was reserved for Joe Frazier. While Frazier originally supported Ali's cause after Ali was stripped of his title, their relationship would soon switch to outright hatred, especially from Frazier's point of view. Ali, in gearing up for the first match, uses racial epithets in describing Frazier, declaring him an Uncle Tom. As one Ali corner man would say later, Frazier was a raging black, forced to leave his native South Carolina due to trouble with local whites. When he was not calling Frazier an Uncle Tom, he was calling Frazier stupid and ugly. Later Ali would claim this was to draw attendance, but Joe Frazier viewed this attack personally. His children would feel the brunt of Ali's attacks with attacks on themselves from their school buddies. For Frazier, defeating Ali was more than keeping his championship, it was about restoring his honor.

The first fight was a brutal affair with both men in the hospital after it was over. Ali began the fight quickly and dominated the early rounds. Frazier took control after the third round, dominating with a vicious body attack followed by thunderous left hooks. Ali came back in the 9th round to win that round with massive punches to Frazier's face but the 11th saw Frazier nearly ending the fight with a left hook. Ali took the 14th but Frazier knocked Ali down in the 15th with a left hook wound up from South Carolina. Ali finished the fight on his feet but Frazier won the first fight in their trilogy. For Frazier, this was his high point as a fighter. He was never better against possibly the greatest fighter ever, and he would never again reach these heights.

Frazier won the fight, but somehow Ali won the crowd. For many, it was a defeat that signified the victory of the establishment. Within the shadow of the Vietnam conflict and the onset of the Nixon era, this fight was more than a sporting event, it reflected the divide of the society as a whole. Frazier was caricatured as the protegee of the establishment, and his victory would taint him as a tool of White America. Both fighters would continue with their careers but Ali would continue to overshadow Frazier in defeat as in victory.

Frazier would beat a couple of stiffs before losing his championship to George Foreman. Frazier was not strong enough to handle the heavy punching Foreman. His second fight with Ali was seen at the time as a battle between two washed up champions. The fight lacked the sizzle of either the first or third fight, but seen today, it merely prepared us for the final act between these two men. Ali started this fight similar to his other fights by dominating the early rounds. He almost knocked Frazier out in the second and won the decision.

Ali then upset George Foreman in the "rumble in the jungle." Using his tactical skills, Ali had Dundee loosen the ropes. Borrowing a page from the old Mongoose, Archie Moore, adopted his rope-a-dope. Foreman punched himself out and Ali finished off the young slugger.

With this background, the third fight promised to be a quick night for Ali. Frazier was considered over the hill and no match for Ali. The drama that preceeded the first fight was not there, though the match proved to be even more brutal, possibly the most brutal heavyweight championship fight in history. For both of these men, this fight was not about the championship; it was about the control of each other. For Frazier, he meant to beat Ali or die trying and he almost got his wish.

The fight followed the pattern of the other fights. Ali started out fast, hitting Frazier with every imaginable combination. Frazier, starting in the fifth round, dominated the middle rounds with some of the most vicious body punches seen in Heavyweight history. By the 10th round, Ali could barely return to his corner and Frazier was on his a to victory. In every fighter's career, there is that moment a fighter goes beyond the pale to find what's deep in his reservoir. Ali in the 12th round, came out with one last rally, hitting Frazier with combinations to Smokin' Joe's face. Frazier left eye closed and now he was vulnerable to Ali's right. In the 13th, Frazier's mouthpiece ended up in the seventh row and by the 14th, Ali was hitting Frazier at will. Kram, covering the match for SI, counted nearly 30 right hooks finding their target on Frazier's face. Eddie Futch, Frazier's long time corner man, stopped the fight. He could no longer stand his fighter's plight and refused to allow any more torture. Frazier would never forgive his corner man for this but Futch was right. Neither man had much left. The Trilogy ended.

Ali continued to reign as champ for nearly three years, but was not the same fighter. He barely escaped with a decision over Ken Norton that could have gone the other way, and was punished by Ernie Shavers before winning that fight. He managed to win his title back a third time from a non-descript Leon Spinks before retiring. His subsequent comeback against Larry Holmes ended in humiliation. His final misguided effort was a loss to Trevor Bobick.

Joe Frazier's own career ended shortly as well. George Foreman pounded the proud gladiator during the American bicentennial celebration and then five years later; Frazier fought some pug to a draw.

Today, Ali suffers from Parkinson's Disease-a direct result of his boxing career. He is but a shadow of his former self. As for Frazier, the bitterness of fighting in Ali's shadow, and the torment he suffered from his rival, still stings. A champion in his own right, he is a survivor. But in many ways, he is a tragic figure; denied his status as a great heavyweight. Ali's recognition would not have occurred without his classic battles against Frazier and Foreman. Kram dismisses Ali as a voice of a new generation but he cannot dismiss Ali's greatness within the ring itself. Frazier was a great fighter in his own right but Ali was the greatest to wear a boxing glove. Frazier's curse is that he boxed in the shadow of another man's greatness. Ali's curse was that his career was sacrificed, in part, to causes for which he had only a rudimentary understanding. For both men, there is nothing but permanent scars. Ali shuffles like an old man, his brash rap reduced to a stammering mumble. Frazier's bitterness is still palpable, as much a fixture of his retirement as it was of his career. Both men represented the artistry and brutality of their sport, leaving nothing back in the ring and paying the price with their broken lives. For the rest of us, their struggles, human and pugilistic, are an epic that reaches beyond boxing.

Ali-Frazier: Golden Age of Boxing

TODAY IS THE MOST IMPORTANT DATE IN THE HISTORY OF THE WORLD....... BAR NONE
March 8, 1971 was the day the world stopped. It was the day the sports world would change forever. It was the day an 11-year-old kid's life changed and would never be the same again.
For this is the day that an 11-year-old kid sat on the floor at 108 Ardmore Ave in Haddonfield N.J. 08033 reading the Courier Post about that night's big Fight. This pimpled face kid counted down the minutes, and kept asking his father who he thought would win tonight. This would go on to become Christmas Eve, Easter Sunday, And New Years eve for this school-skipping brat. This is the Night that Ali and Frazier came to blows, and put on a fight for all-time between two of the six greatest Heavyweights who have yet lived.
Frank Lotierzo March 8, 2002

The Unforgettable Fire of Smokin' Joe

By Frank J. Lotierzo
Published October Wail, Cyberboxing.com

During the final countdown of the past millennium, we had been subjected to an overwhelming number of Top Ten lists. I had paid particular attention to the lists ranking history's top ten greatest heavyweight champions.

After reviewing several boxing publications, internet sites and conducting a personal survey of writers and trainers, I found two irrefutable parallels: (1) Muhammad Ali and Joe Louis were named one and two a majority of the time and (2) Joe Frazier was often found in the bottom third and consistently behind Jack Dempsey and Rocky Marciano. The names Holyfield and Tyson were usually above Frazier as well.

I found myself wondering if the individuals who ranked these fighters saw the same Joe Frazier I did during the years 1968 through 1974. Perhaps ABC replayed Frazier-Foreman I so many times that Howard Cosell's call of "Down goes Frazier, down goes Frazier, down goes Frazier" is what most remember when recalling the career of Smokin' Joe. Maybe the overwhelming presence of Muhammad Ali during the 70's and the emergence of the colorful George Foreman of the 90's have overshadowed the accomplishments of Frazier's renowned boxing career.

Looking back at Frazier's career, several things stand out. He was without peer as a body puncher. He fought with never-ending stamina and became stronger as the fight progressed. He cut off the ring and forced his opponents to fight his fight at his pace, possessing a left hook that was without equal in the heavyweight division. Frazier's record is a virtual list of the top heavies of the late 60's through the mid-70's. As early as his 11th pro bout, he took on the "Argentine Bull," Oscar Bonavena a veteran of over 30 fights as a pro. After being down twice in the 2nd Round, Frazier stormed back to win the hard-fought 10 Round decision. He was the first to stop the iron-chinned Jerry Quarry and the reigning WBA Heavyweight Champion Jimmy Ellis. Frazier will always be remembered as the first fighter to defeat Muhammad Ali in the biggest and most highly anticipated fight in history. It has been said Frazier won because Ali had just returned to the ring after a 43-month layoff. What is sadly overlooked is that Ali was still a great fighter and fought one of the best fights of his career that night. Frazier's strength, aggression and determination made it impossible for Ali to fight at anything but his best, or Frazier would have half killed him. Had Ali fought anyone except Joe Frazier that night, he would have been a knockout winner. Let's not forget that Frazier was no walk in the park for Ali in their second fight and that he had Ali thinking "No Mas" after the 10th Round of their third and most grueling fight in Manila. Ali has been quoted as saying Frazier was the roughest and toughest fighter he ever faced in the ring. No one can deny the fact that Ali fought the world's top heavyweights from 1960 through 1980. Shouldn't his opinion count for something when evaluating Frazier? He fought more rounds against him than any other fighter.

Over the years Smokin' Joe has been criticized because he never fought any big punchers other than George Foreman. My retort to that is, unless you are talking Baer, Louis or Shavers, every other fighter looks like Slapsie Maxie if Foreman is the measuring stick. Manuel Ramos stood 6' 3", weighed 230 pounds and had a pulverizing right uppercut that Frazier walked through on his way to scoring a 2nd Round knockout. Oscar Bonavena was a 6' 210 pound wall of granite. In their second fight, with Frazier's title on the line, Frazier cruised to victory, winning almost all of the 15 round fight on the judges' cards.

Jerry Quarry was a good enough puncher that the 6'3" Ron Lyle retreated after being hit with Quarry's bombs, and Earnie Shavers could not get out of the 1st Round with Quarry. Frazier stood up to the hardest punches Quarry ever landed and kept coming forward and wearing Quarry down. Joe repeated his performance more thoroughly five years later when they met a second time. How about Ali? Ali hit hard enough to be the first to stop Liston, and Lyle and was the only one to stop Bonavena and Foreman. The rugged Chuck Wepner was knocked down only once, this accomplished by Ali-something Liston and Foreman could not do. Joe Frazier, over the course of three fights, spent 41 grueling rounds in the ring with Ali. During that time Ali hit Frazier with some of the swiftest combinations and hardest punches he ever hit any opponent with and did not knock him down. The only time Frazier was stopped by Ali was in the Manila fight. His eye was completely swollen shut and he was getting hit with punches he could not see.

Frazier's title tenure lasted five years. He made ten successful defenses, winning eight by knockout. He lost the title to Foreman and failed to regain it from Ali. Some of the fighters who were often ranked higher than Frazier lost their titles to fighters who on their best day would be honored to pay their way into the gym just to see him shadow box. Mike Tyson was stripped of his title by a journeyman named Buster Douglas. Michael Moorer, a fat light heavyweight, dethroned Evander Holyfield and, Michael Spinks, a manufactured heavyweight, beat Larry Holmes. You do not need me to tell you that Douglas, Moorer and Spinks would have had more than their feelings hurt had they attempted to take Frazier's title.

Two fighters Frazier is most unfavorably compared to are Jack Dempsey and Rocky Marciano. Who did they fight anywhere near the caliber of Ali or Foreman? How do we know how Dempsey and Marciano would have fared had they fought the Foreman of 1973-74? Don't be misled that it is a foregone conclusion either one of them would have been victorious. Dempsey was knocked out in the 1st

Round by Fireman Jim Flynn and knocked out of the ring by Luis Firpo. A left hook courtesy of 38-year old Jersey Joe Walcott dropped Marciano, and 40-something Light Heavyweight Champ Archie Moore put Rocky down. Is it a reach to think Foreman would have defeated Dempsey and Marciano? The same Foreman who helped make Frazier a former champ? Not one bit!

Over the years many blanket statements have been made diminishing Frazier's accomplishments because of the way he lost to Foreman. I have this to say to those who have admonished him. Foreman is not just another puncher. He came back and won the title at age 45 with a one-punch knockout.

Foreman throws arm punches and has knocked out fighters from 1969 through 1995. Boxing has never seen such a monstrosity, before or since. Dempsey, Marciano. Holmes, Tyson and Holyfield have never shared a ring with a fighter who is in the same zip code as Foreman in punching power. Holyfield barely survived his fight with him when Foreman was 42.

After thoroughly and objectively reviewing Frazier's career, it is abundantly clear that to beat him you had to be a great fighter. Two fighters can claim victory over Frazier, George Foreman, the most powerful heavyweight in the last hundred years and maybe ever, and Muhammad Ali, the most skilled, and widely accepted as the greatest heavyweight ever. Ali is a legend today because of his victory over Foreman. You can't have it both ways.

Norton Speaks on Fights
with Ali

By Frank J.Lotierzo

o o o o o o o o o o o o o o o o o o o o o o o o o o o o o

Recently I had the pleasure of speaking with former Heavyweight Champion Ken Norton on my radio show "Toe to Toe" heard on ESPN Radio 1490. Ken was in town with his newly published book titled "Going the Distance." I must tell you that I have read many books written by fighters and this is one of the best. It is insightful, informative and a definite must-read. Ken gave me almost an hour of his time. We cannot provide you with the entire interview due to time and space restrictions.

Ken Norton is best known for breaking Muhammad Ali's jaw in a stunning upset on March 31, 1973. Ali and Norton would meet two more times with Ali winning each time by a controversial decision. Here are Ken Norton's thoughts on all three historic bouts.

——Frank Lotierzo

Frank: "Kenny, Muhammad Ali is held in such high esteem today because of all the great fighters he fought. You and Joe Frazier are the only two fighters he fought three times. Can you tell us why you were chosen to fight Ali the first time?"

Norton: "I fought on the Ali-Bob Foster under card against Henry Clark. After the fights, he was down in the bar or lounge area with a bunch of ladies. I came down and kinda stole part of his thunder. He jumped up and said I'm gonna to box you and started yelling I'm gonna kick your butt. So that was the beginning of the end for Ali."

Frank: "What were you ranked at that time?"

Norton: "Seventh by Ring Magazine."

Frank: "You were a 7 to 1 underdog going into that first fight with Ali. You fought him as if you were the favorite. What was it about him that made you so confident you could beat him?"

Norton: "Bob Foster told me after his fight with Ali, he came up and said you can take him. I knew I would beat him because mentally I felt that way and my whole camp felt that way. I felt at that time I could've beat Godzilla."

Frank: "Of all the fighters Ali has beaten, you are the only one he never beat convincingly"

Norton: "A lot of it was the mental part of it. Ali defeated everyone mentally first. With Frazier, Ali had him so mad, Joe was trying to kill him with every shot. With Foreman, he tried to kill Ali with every shot. Mentally, Ali could not defeat me and physically, I felt I was as much a physical power as Ali was. He couldn't upset me in any way and plus, I had Eddie Futch. Eddie knew how to fight Ali. You can't go the head with him. You have to go the body first and then eventually he will bring his hands down and lower his head."

Frank: "Over the years there has been much speculation as to which round you broke his jaw in. Feddie Pacheco, who was Ali's doctor at that time, said it was broken during the second round. What round do you believe it was?

Norton: "Round 12. Ali had a break that was an inch and half long and you keep getting hit as hard and as much as I hit Ali, the pain would take over and you would pass out."

Frank: "Which one of your three fights with Ali, do you think you fought your best?"

Norton: "I would say that the one I fought the best was the last one at Yankee Stadium. After 15 rounds, I was not tired and felt I could've fought 15 more."

Frank: "Which fight did Ali fight the best of the three?"

Norton: "Ali, I would say the second fight for him."

Frank: Which of the three fights do you think was the closest?

Norton: "I would say the second."

Frank: "Do you think Ali stole the second fight by winning the 12th round with his big flurries in that round?'

Norton: "Yes. Ali was bigger than boxing at that time."

Frank: "It is fair to say that Ali won the second fight by winning the last round and that's why he won the decision?"

Norton: "Yes, I can see why they gave him the decision."

Frank: "In your third fight, which was for Ali's title, it came down to the 15th round on the judges' scorecards. All three scored the round for Ali. What was your thinking at that time going into that 15th round?"

Norton: "I was told by my trainer, at the time which was Bill Clayton that I was ahead on points. He said don't go out and get cut, don't go out and get hurt, just go out and control the round and watch yourself and be careful. I went out and thought I did enough to have a draw in that round."

Frank: If you could fight that round again, how would you fight it?

Norton: "I would fight it like I fought the other 14. I would just go out and win it. Like I said, I could've fought 15 more rounds."

Frank: "In your book, you said after the third fight with Ali went against you, you lost your heart for boxing, but you continued boxing. Why?"

Norton: "I lost my edge for boxing, I didn't put as much into it as I did before. I didn't run as far. I didn't train as hard. I didn't train correctly. I started drinking a little bit every now and then. On a scale of 1 to 10, I put it about 5. I felt no matter what I did they would do what they want anyway."

Frank: "In other words, unless you scored a knockout you weren't going to get the decision."

Norton: "Right. This is not to take away anything from Larry Holmes who I fought after that, but if I trained for Larry the same way I trained for Ali, I felt I could've done quite a bit better."

Frank: In your book you say Ali is the best ever. Do you believe that?

Norton: "As far as I've been around, yes."

Frank: Is Ali the best fighter you ever fought?

Norton: "Yes."

Frank: "You also said in your book that you and Ali are good friends today. It is true that he was one of the first to come and see you in the hospital after your terrible car accident in 1986."

Norton: "That's very true."

What Ali Had!

By Frank J. Lotierzo

What did Muhammad Ali possess that allowed him to defeat Smokin' Joe Frazier in two out of three fights? What was that one weapon he possessed that enabled him to prevail? It is something that is overlooked when evaluating the three classic fights between these two former all-time great Heavyweight Champions. When thinking back to sports greatest rivalry, it is easy to overlook the one factor, which would determine who history would regard as the better fighter. The difference maker in these three fights came down to the overall abundance of body strength and durability of Muhammad Ali. Throw out his hand speed and lightning fast combinations, the great footwork, the overall ability to adapt on the fly, and the tremendous psychological warfare Ali could employ. The bottom line is that Ali had a cast iron chin, complemented by a concrete body and very under rated physical body strength. Not one of the gaudy weapons Ali displayed physically mattered in victory. It was the weapons we couldn't see until the terms warranted them to be brought out and shown to us. Bottom line, Ali could absorb Frazier's relentless assault.

Can you picture any boxer other than Ali surviving Joe Frazier? I can't! He is the perfect foil for a boxer. Here's the problem with a boxer trying to survive Frazier. He wouldn't allow boxers to box him. He puts unrelenting pressure on them, which forces them to fight him instead of boxing him. The Heavyweight division has yet to deliver a boxer other than Ali, who can take the pressure and fight back. Regardless how skillful the boxer was, boxing fundamentals go out the window. The other problem boxers' face was Frazier coming in bobbing and weaving. He would hit you to the body or the head; there isn't a safe place in the ring. His punches to the body sapped your strength and his left hook separated your head from the rest of your body. He would cut off your space and punching distance while closing in to position himself so he could thoroughly work you over. He had a great chin. Eventually Frazier wore his opponent down. Frazier's opponents found themselves looking to the referee for aid.

Look what Frazier did to some very good boxers. Buster Mathis was big and had the feet of a ballet dancer, and he had fast hands. Mathis had the mental advantage of beating Frazier twice in the box-off for a birth on the 1964 Olympic team. They fought four years later for the New York State Heavyweight title. History would show that Mathis had three beautiful opening rounds and then Frazier took command before knocking out Mathis in the eleventh. This was typical of Frazier's fights. Mathis started off moving and jabbing, trying to keep Frazier at a distance. Mathis was trying to box and keep Frazier from pinning him against the rope, but paid a heavy price. Frazier forced Mathis to use up his strength and energy by the minute. One other subtle thing happened, Mathis was losing his will. The longer the fight went the more damage was done. Two minutes into the eleventh round, the end came in classic Frazier fashion as he dug a hook to the body, taking Mathis' air and legs. A second hook ended the fight as Mathis dropped to the canvas as though he was dropped from a helicopter.

On June 23, 1969, Joe Frazier defended his title against the second ranked heavyweight in the world, counterpunching Jerry Quarry. Quarry was finding out that you couldn't counterpunch the non-stop pressure and continuous punching by Frazier. Being forced to fight the first two rounds, Quarry got the better of Joe. By the fifth round, Quarry found himself pinned against the ropes with not a whole lot left in his gas tank to keep Frazier from working him over. Broadcaster Howard Cosell called Angelo Dundee (who was sitting ringside with WBA Champ Jimmy Ellis) over to the broadcast booth, and asked, "Alright, Angie, lets hear once and for all, is your man going to meet

Frazier." Dundee replied, "Jimmy will be happy to meet Frazier, I assure you he won't have his back to the ropes like that." Oh how wrong he was.

Quarry was not on the ropes because he chose to be, Frazier had taken his legs and Quarry could not escape. On February 16, 1970, Frazier and Ellis met for the undisputed Heavyweight title. Ellis, a cute boxer with a sneaky stiff right hand, won the first two rounds. Frazier was getting closer each minute of the fight. Midway through round three, Frazier caught Ellis with a brutal left hook to the chin and Ellis wobbled for a brief second. At the end of the round, Ellis was pinned against the ropes and Frazier started landing body punches. When the bell rang ending the third round, Ellis returned to his corner a different man.

In round four, Frazier took command and ended the fight. Frazier pinned Ellis to the ropes, and once again landed hooks to the body and head. Ellis crumbled to the floor. Ellis had tremendous heart and rose at the count of five. Frazier met Ellis in the center of the ring after the first knockdown crashing Ellis with hooks to the body and head. Frazier dipped and came up with a left hook and Ellis was down. (This left hook was the second best left hook I have ever seen in a heavyweight fight, the best being the left hook that dropped Ali in their first fight.) Ellis climbed up and struggled back to his corner, where Dundee took mercy and stopped the fight. Frazier would repeat this victory over Ellis five years later, when they met for a rematch. Frazier was preparing for the third Ali fight and wore Ellis down, to win in nine rounds. In case it has not sunk in yet, Ali had a cast iron chin, concrete body, underrated physical strength and determination equal to Frazier. He had these extra qualities that other boxers did not have.

The proof, Frazier-Ali I. Ali came out extremely fast, throwing the hardest punches he had ever thrown at any opponent in rounds one thru five. His plan was to get Frazier out and he didn't, Frazier would take so much punishment that he wouldn't be effective in the last third of the fight. As we know, Frazier was stunned pretty good in those rounds but they also took a toll on Ali. Ali found out that there was no half-court game with Joe Frazier, that it is a fast break all the way. In rounds six, seven, and eight, Ali was now flatfooted and had to endure the relentless Frazier's assault. Ali summoned great reserve and had a big round in the ninth, stunning Frazier in the last twenty seconds to have his last big round. Round 10 was close, with Frazier gaining a slight advantage. In round eleven, Ali came close to being stopped. Midway through the round, Frazier connects with a double left hook to the body and head. Ali was in the dream room and he counted upon his body strength and iron cast chin to survive the round. Frazier worked Ali's body and head over the next two rounds. Ali rallies in the fourteenth but twenty-four seconds into round fifteen, Frazier connected with the fiercest left hook I ever witnessed in the heavyweight division. Ali goes down as if his legs were taken out from under him, but got up at the count of two. Cast iron chin! Frazier worked his body and head for the remainder of the round. Ali survived the round but lost a unanimous decision. He survived because of his cast iron chin, concrete body and unmatched physical strength.

The second Ali-Frazier once again showed Ali's concrete chin and physical strength. Ali came out moving and circling, forcing Frazier to chase more than stalk. Ali could not do this for the whole fight. Ali took four of the first six rounds. Rounds seven and eight, Frazier started smokin' as Ali needed a rest. Ali was too tired to move and had no choice but to lean against the ropes and endure Joe's bombs. Again, concrete body, and cast iron chin allowed Ali to remain on his feet. When the body started hurting, Ali called on his physical strength to grab Frazier. By tying Frazier, Ali prevented further damage. Ali took the ninth and eleventh rounds to take the lead, going into the final round.

Frazier, sensing that he needed a big round in the final stanza, came out to kill Ali. Frazier landed some big hooks to Ali's chin early in the round but Ali's recuperative powers came to life and Ali finished the round with a big flurry—taking the decision.

The Thrilla in Manila repeated the pattern of the previous two fights. Ali started quickly, shaking Frazier in rounds one and two. The pace slowed a little in rounds three and four, with Ali picking his spots and scoring clean punches. Frazier took round five as he started getting inside and working Ali's body. Frazier finished the round with an exploding left hook to Ali's chin. Round six saw Frazier landing his calling card, his left hook. Ali was stopped in his tracks. Ali's recuperative powers allowed him to come back in round seven taking the round by jabbing cleanly. Ali continued in round eight, scoring heavily but in the next two rounds Frazier took command. Frazier whacked Ali from corner to corner. After the tenth, Ali looked like a beaten and dejected fighter. Halfway through the eleventh, Ali got his second or even third wind and started fighting Frazier on even ground, winning a close round. In round twelve, Ali displayed to the audience the unbelievable strength needed to grab Frazier and literally push Frazier off of him and at the same time starting to land his own heavy artillery. By the end of the twelfth round, Frazier looked the way most of his opponents look after a grueling fight with him. Ali then got his fourth and fifth wind and was now cleaning up on Frazier with accurate stinging combinations, which seemed almost impossible after enduring one of the most brutal body attacks ever seen in the heavyweight division. After knocking out Frazier's mouthpiece in the fourteenth, Ali finally took command. With Frazier's eyes almost swollen shut, his trainer Eddie Futch stopped the fight and saved Frazier from taking further punishment.

How did Ali do this? The reason Ali survived Frazier was because Ali had the best chin of any heavyweight champion. His overall body strength was grossly underrated. Look at the way he could tie up Frazier, Foreman and Liston keeping them from doing anything but wait for the referee to break them apart. Do you have any concept how much this strength enabled Ali to survive and defeat these sluggers? If Ali's strength and chin were less, he would have been 0-3 against Frazier. No way would he have withstood the onslaught of Liston and

Foreman as well. That is why Ali is the greatest champion who ever walked the earth. Cast iron chin, a concrete body that could withstand unbelievable body shots and tremendous physical body strength allowed him to give out more than he took in. What a fighting machine! Not only was Ali gifted with never before seen physical skills seen in a heavyweight before him, but was wrapped with the toughness and determination of a Greb or Marciano, and even a Joe Frazier. Muhammad Ali had more weapons and ways to beat great fighters than any other Heavyweight Champion in history. Muhammad Ali could have defeated any other Heavyweight Champion in history if they were to meet. That's not up for conjecture.

Patterson, Unsung Crusader

By Tom Donelson

Floyd Patterson was an enigma; a fighter who did not have the big punch or size needed to be a great heavyweight champion but found himself an unwilling representative (sometimes) in the growing debate on civil rights in the early 60's. Armed with the quick hands of a middleweight and cursed with a glass chin, Patterson found himself vulnerable to the better heavyweights of his day, including Ali and Liston.

According to Gerald Early, Floyd Patterson along with Jose Torres ranked as "one of the most thoughtful fighters ever to enter the boxing ring." Such traits are rarely seen in a fighter and some would even see it as a hindrance. Cus D' Amato observed about his own fight early in Patterson's career, "Patterson lacked the killer instinct. He's too tame, too nice to his opponents." The difference between Patterson the philosopher, and Liston the street man, was summarized in an interview conducted by Howard Cosell before their first fight. Patterson appeared to be lecturing Liston about the responsibility of the heavyweight crown during the interview. When Cosell asked Liston about his view of Patterson, Liston prophetically responded, "I just want to run him over with a truck." He did so in short order, knocking out Patterson in the first round. Patterson came into the heavyweight division as the Division was changing. Sonny Liston was a big puncher, who weighed over 215 pounds. Ali combined size with athleticism. After Patterson, no heavyweight fighter would ever weigh less than 200 pounds. Patterson was the last heavyweight fighter under 200 pounds and he did not even reach 190 pounds when he won the heavyweight title.

Early wrote that Patterson viewed Ali or the man he called Cassius Clay, "as alter ego… Perhaps Ali was the fighter that he, Patterson, always aspired to be." Patterson stated in a Sports Illustrated article that if he moved and jabbed as opposed to moving straight into Liston's power range, he would have won. I remember watching Patterson's victory over George Chuvalo, in which Patterson imitated Ali as he moved and danced. This fight set up the Patterson-Ali fight in which Ali would easily win. I marveled at Patterson's hand speed but he seemed dwarfed by the Canadian pugilist, with this remaining the core of Patterson's problem as a heavyweight. He just was not big enough nor had a power punch to compensate for his smaller frame.

Patterson was also caught in the racial storm raging around him. Patterson was a black Roman Catholic, whereas most African-Americans stayed with their Baptist evangelical roots. Patterson believed in the melting pot and for him, his heavyweight belt was his chance to talk about the value of sports and be a role model for young people, and young blacks, in particular.

After beating Archie Moore for the Heavyweight Championship, Patterson fought a series of non-descript fighters, mostly white. Sonny Liston revealed to one of his biographers that one of his reasons for disliking Patterson was because "he hasn't fought any colored boys since becoming champion. Patterson draws the color line against his own race. We have a hard enough time as it is in a white man's world." Worthy black fighters such as Cleveland Williams, and Zora Folley had to wait until Ali became champion before receiving their shot at the title. The only black that received a shot at the title was an erratic heavyweight named "Hurricane" Jackson. Other challengers included Olympic champion Pete Rademacher in his first professional fight and the hapless Tom McNeeley. The only worthy white opponent that Patterson fought was Ingemar Johannson.

Patterson entered his first fight with Johannson full of confidence, but the bigger Johannson slaughtered Patterson with seven knockdowns in the third round. Johannson, a typical European fighter fought straight up, and had a powerful right hand that he called "Thor." "Thor" found Patterson routinely in the third round, and Johannson became the last white heavyweight fighter to hold the unified heavyweight title. Patterson felt that he let America down and as he told Peter Heller in an interview, "Losing a championship is bad enough, but losing it to a foreigner was even worse." For Patterson, these sentiments reflected a need to be recognized as an American at a time in which many blacks were denied basic civil rights in most places in the United States.

Patterson would redeem himself, becoming the first heavyweight to regain his championship with a vicious left hook that knocked the Swede unconscious. Seeing film of that knockout leaves me with shivers. Johannson lay on the ground, with just his feet moving and the rest of his body limped. The hapless Johannson looked dead. This would be Patterson's finest moment as he demonstrated the needed killer instinct that he rarely showed before or since. For Patterson, beating Johannson was not racial but personal. He felt humiliated at being knocked down seven times the first fight and now revenged his loss and redeemed himself. Patterson would win the rubber match and then defeat the hapless Tom McNeeley before meeting Liston.

Patterson was everybody's hero when he allowed Liston to fight for his title. Liston was a mob-controlled fighter, who acted the part of mob goon when he was not in the boxing ring. Patterson found himself in a battle of good vs. evil as he stepped into the ring against Liston. Patterson recalled the pressure, "The President of the United States, Ralph Bunche, all the celebrities, all the big leaders of the country, all the millions of letters I received, they made Liston the bad guy and I was the good guy." Patterson was the defender of what was right with America. Gerald Early writes that Patterson was the defender of bourgeois black life in white America at a time that some blacks were challenging the bourgeois life style. Patterson began to feel the weight of a messianic duty, a burden that he could not mentally or physically handle. He admitted, "I don't ever want to endure that kind of pressure again. To me, fighting is fighting. It's a sport." President Kennedy pleaded with Patterson to "keep the championship."

Liston massacred Patterson, twice. He did not have the power or the size to fight Liston, and even if he boxed Liston, he would not have won. These fights impacted Patterson's own standing, as Gerald Early reported that his standing within the black community started to deteriorate.

While many Black Leaders considered him a hero in fighting the evil Liston; younger black activists attacked him as a pathetic "Uncle Tom" when he condemned Ali in two pieces for Sports Illustrated. Early observed that Patterson's opposition to Ali was akin to "an outraged middle-class black who finds that his lower-class cousin has gone balmy over some sort of storefront charlatanism." But Early conceded, "his basic instincts about the inadequacy of the Muslim response to American racism proved to be generally correct."

Patterson refused to acknowledge Ali's Muslim beliefs by continuing to call him by his Christian name Cassius Clay, and approached his fight with Ali like a crusade. Ali, in return, treated this fight as a jihad and with his superior skills tortured and taunted the smaller Patterson. Throughout the fight, Ali slapped accurate sharp jabs in Patterson's face. When it appeared that Patterson was ready to go, Ali would ease up with the goal of keeping Patterson around for one more round-one more round to torment the black Catholic. This fight resembled less a boxing match and more a religious crusade—but this debate was one-sided.

Seven years later, Patterson would get one more chance at Ali, but by this time Ali's own view had mellowed. No longer needing to torture or humiliate his Christian nemesis, Ali finished Patterson off more quickly in seven rounds.

Patterson was trapped between two black cultures, the slowly emerging middle class that now predominates the African-American community today and the more radical black separatists—who drifted toward Ali. Later, Joe Frazier would replace Patterson in the eyes of many in the radical black arena as the new "White Champion." Unlike Patterson, Frazier never sought to be leader of any crusade and he was all "raging black." And, unlike Patterson, Frazier had the power to cause Ali damage. Frazier's Trilogy with Ali was a classic in the history of boxing, with Frazier giving as much as he received from Ali.

Floyd Patterson was a transitional fighter in boxing history, a fighter who stood for a middle class black society that was—and is still—invisible to many Americans. His small stature and inability to defeat his two major nemeses diminished his stature within boxing history. He could not defeat the mob-controlled Liston or the brash Ali. This thinking heavyweight was limited by his natural handicaps to control his destiny and represent his cause in the ring.

Harry Wills, Shot for Glory Denied

By Tom Donelson

Between 1915 and 1927, Harry Wills was one of the best fighters, if not the best, in the heavyweight division. Yet, he never got his chance to fight for the heavyweight championship. Like other black fighters in the early part of the past century, Harry Wills is nothing but a footnote in boxing history. What denied Wills his place in history was the color of his skin. At a time in which the heavyweight championship was considered the purview of the Caucasian race, Harry Wills tilled in the hinterland of the heavyweight division. After Jack Johnson's reign as champion ended, white promoters were determined not to allow blacks a whiff of the championship belt.

Jack Johnson's personal conduct outside the ring scandalized White America as modesty and humility were not part of his make up. Jack Johnson essentially gave White America the middle finger as he violated every taboo of his time. Jack Johnson found white women more to his liking as he said, "Every colored lady I ever went with two-timed me, white girls didn't." And when he was not bedding white women, he was beating white heavyweights. He did not just beat his opponent; he taunted and tortured them before beating them. Ring Lardner described Jack Johnson as that "grinning Negro whose delight was in whipping Caucasian fighters with taunts pouring from his mouth." Forced into exile due to the Mann Act, which outlawed "taking women across state line for immoral purpose", Johnson spent the last years of his championship reign outside the country. He eventually lost his title to Jess Willard under the scorching Havana sun.

Harry Wills came into his own as a fighter after Johnson relinquished his title in 1915. A strong and big fighter for his era, Harry Wills used his size as an advantage. Black boxing historian Keith Smith told me in an EMAIL interview that Harry Wills' skills, "would be considered good for his day. His strength was his asset. He could move other men around the ring as he pleased. He could then put them in position and land as he saw fit. He was a master of holding and hitting (which in the teens was considered an art form and not frowned upon as much as it is today)." An athletic man for his size with one punch knock out power, Wills dominated most of the heavyweight division.

Smith considered Wills one of the best between 1915-1922. As he declared, "Besides Dempsey, and an old (but still great) Langford, I can't see anyone who would be considered a favorite over Wills." In 1919, Jess Willard decided to put his championship up for grabs. As the Great White Hope who ended the Johnson championship reign, Jess Willard was America's hero. At the age of 37 and having fought only once over the previous four years since defeating Jack Johnson, Willard was ripe for the picking. As with many fighters in the early part of the century, there are many debates about Willard's boxing skills. There are very few films to truly judge Willard, so we only have second hand accounts gathered through the oral history of past boxing historians as well as newspaper accounts. Nat Fleischer considered Willard, "one of the poorest of the heavyweight champions.... Jess was a slow moving pugilist who disliked training as much as he disliked the sport." Seymour Rothman of the Toledo Blade provided another point of view when he wrote that Willard "was truly equipped to be a champion. He had a long left arm, which held off eager opponents. His right hand punches were devastating." Willard's size and endurance were his major assets.

Tex Rickard, the major boxing promoter from 1910 till his death in 1929, told his financial backers that he would never match Willard with a black fighter. Roger Kahn noted that for Rickard, the issue was as much about money as racism. Kahn quoted Rickard telling one of his financial backers, "if a nigger wins the championship, then the championship isn't worth a nickel." This reasoning eliminated both Sam Langford and Harry Wills. By this time, Langford was past his prime but Wills was at his peak as a fighter. His strength and durability would have made the Willard-Wills fight an interesting proposition. As Kevin Smith told me, "When you meet Sam Langford 18 times over and live to tell about it—you are a serious fighter. I guess it can best be said that Harry Wills was legit. He had size, speed, power, a bit of grace, and a great deal of experience." Rickard denied Wills his first chance at the heavyweight title. While Kahn would write that Rickard's major concern was making money, he added that with Rickard, "the issue was money, not prejudice. Or anyway money before prejudice." Rickard's racism played a role in denying Wills his shot at the championship throughout his career. (Rickard's impact can't be underestimated. Rickard's control of the sport in the 20's would make modern day promoters Don King and Bob Arum envious.)

After racism eliminated Wills from contention, it created Jack Dempsey's date with destiny as he destroyed Willard over three rounds in a display of ferocity rarely seen in heavyweight fighting. As Dempsey ruled the heavyweight division, beating what was left of white contenders, Wills toiled unknown to the white boxing audience. With no more legitimate white heavyweights left, Jack Dempsey decided to take a break from fighting in 1923. The only contenders left were a light heavyweight named Gene Tunney and Harry Wills. Wills, unfortunately, had another opponent—age.

Roger Kahn makes it clear in his autobiography that Jack Dempsey was willing to fight Harry Wills. Dempsey signed contracts to fight Wills on two different occasions but reneged when finances failed to materialize. Roger Kahn noted about Dempsey, "Not awed by Wills, Dempsey was afraid of something else: boxing without getting paid." Wills, six years older than Dempsey, was running out of time. Despite being the number one challenger for close to a decade, time was eroding Wills' skills. The age factor started showing up when he lost to

Sharkey and barely beat a raw Luis Firpo. Smith pointed out; "Wills was past his prime when he fought Sharkey and pretty much there against Firpo." His loss to Sharkey and Basque contender Paolina Uzcudun in 1927 ended his chances for a title shot. In particular, his loss to Sharkey gave white promoters an excuse to end Wills' quest for the title. His narrow victory over Firpo merely confirmed in the minds of white writers and boxing analysts that Wills did not really deserve a chance at either Tunney or Dempsey. Grantland Rice summed up what most reporters' thought when he wrote about Wills after the Firpo fight, "Wills is not a fighter in Dempsey's class, not even close." (Roger Kahn pointed out in his biography on Jack Dempsey that Tex Rickard had many of the nation's sports writers on his payroll. They merely echoed his thoughts about Wills' inferiority as a boxer.)

While Dempsey never feared Wills, his managers did. Kevin Smith declared," many of the men who ran boxing thought that if Dempsey and Wills fought, the latter would win and that is why the bout never took place. Wills was too much of a threat. "Others are not as sure. Roger Kahn, Dempsey's biographer, stated, "Harry Wills would have proved to be nothing more than another quick Dempsey knockout."

What was lost in this debate is Harry Wills' age. Harry Wills was six years older than Dempsey and as the 1920's began, Wills was already past 30 years of age. Many of the fights that eliminated Wills from serious competition occurred after Wills turned 35. Dempsey always had the advantage of youth on his side. Wills' best years were already behind him and if he proved to be an easy mark for Dempsey, his age would be the key factor. Kevin Smith summed up Wills dilemma when he told me that, "The fact that Harry was black is about the only reason that he never did receive a title shot. He was considered the top contender for almost seven years. No number one contender could be ignored for that long today—but the racial tones of that time simply would not allow such a bout"

Kevin Smith added that Wills was at his best during the late teens and the early 20's. If Dempsey had fought Wills then, it could have been a great fight. Luis Firpo, a fighter similar to Wills, nearly ended Dempsey's reign as champion when he knocked the Manassa Mauler out of the ring. Firpo's eventual loss does not diminish the fact that a Wills-Dempsey bout in 1920 or 1921 would have been a splendid event. Certainly, Dempsey was not invincible, as Tunney would later show. While Dempsey was impressive against Willard, Wills developed his boxing skills by fighting several quality opponents including the great Sam Langford, Sam McVey, and Joe Jeannette.

Harry Wills will be remembered less for the fights that he did fight and more for the championship fight that never happened. It is hard to truly judge Wills ability, since there are very few films of Wills fighting, and we only have second hand reporting to depend upon. Much of this comes from white reporters, who were biased against the black heavyweight from the Big Easy. Racism denied Wills his shot at heavyweight glory. That was the fact.

Byrd Takes Flight at History

By Tom Donelson

Heavyweight contender Jimmy Young briefly boxed his way onto the heavyweight championship scene when he embarrassed Muhammad Ali for 15 rounds in 1976. Young forced an overweight and undertrained Ali to chase him for 15 rounds, and while many boxing observers felt that Young actually delivered the cleaner blows, the judges were not prepared to give this unknown the title. Chris Byrd is today's Jimmy Young.

Jimmy Young, just like Chris Byrd today, was a small heavyweight with a pitty-pat punch. He did not scare you, but he could easily embarrass you. For the next two years, he would fight some of the biggest punchers of his era, winning some and losing some. After Ali, he went on to outpoint both Ron Lyle and George Foreman before losing a heavyweight elimination bout to Ken Norton, thus ending his brief attempt at a championship belt. The one image I had of Jimmy Young was his fight with Foreman. Young, whose strategy involved avoiding heavy contact, was nailed with several vicious shots in the 7th round. Foreman appeared ready for the kill but Young managed to survive the round, mostly on guile and defensive skills. After that, Young came back to outbox Foreman and win the decision. This defeat sent Forman into boxing exile for the next 10 years. Young, if nothing else, demonstrated his toughness, but his lack of punching power ultimately doomed him.

Chris Byrd easily beat Tua in Las Vegas this past fall and demonstrated that small boxers with little power can still be actual contenders for the title. At 6 feet and weighing 215 pounds, Byrd is small by today's heavyweight standards. At the age of 31, his window of opportunity is closing fast, since his skill is based on speed and quickness. He is reaching the time where speed will begin to desert him and leave him exposed without a safety net. Byrd can take a heavyweight beating as his battles with the Klitschko brothers showed, but he can not deliver a heavyweight punch in return. Throughout the Tua fights, he hit Tua with several straight shots that appeared to do little damage, but all night long, he kept throwing punch after punch. Tua appeared more annoyed than hurt but did very little to avoid Byrd's barrages. Tua's heavy-handed body attack did not slow Byrd down and Byrd's conditioning allowed him to escape trouble time and time again.

Byrd is one of the truly nice guys in boxing, the All-American guy who "figuratively speaking" will help little old ladies cross the street. Byrd does not seem to fit the profile of a boxer, a man whose inner demons force him to express his anger in the ring. Boy Scouts tend not to become heavyweight champions, much less contenders.

Chris Byrd may never be a heavyweight champion and his fight with Tua may be his high point, but Byrd has shown a high level of boxing skills and the heart to compete for the title. Just like Jimmy Young two decades earlier, Byrd is a flashing comet, reminding boxing fans that a flashing jab combined with quick feet and fast combinations can bring even the smallest of heavyweights to the pearly gates of championship territory.

The Myth of Plan B December 2001

By Frank J. Lotierzo
Published December Wail, 2001 Cyboxingzone.com

Why didn't he go to Plan B? Because Plan B doesn't exist for fighters whose style it is to move forward. Most of the time when you hear the infamous quote, "Plan B," it refers to a fighter who is a puncher and who was just beaten by a boxer. The list is endless of fights in which the talk the next day is why didn't he adjust .Why didn't Trinidad stop pressing the fight when that tactic clearly wasn't working against Hopkins? Trinidad can only fight effectively going forward; that's how he generates his power. Asking Trinidad not to push the fight is like taking Shaq out of the paint and asking him to beat you with a jump shot! It's not his game and it never will be. The same goes for Trinidad. What would happen to him if he tried to beat Hopkins or DeLaHoya by waiting for them to go to him? He would get taken apart. His style is based on taking advantage of his punching power, which can only be maximized by coming forward. Why do you think when Trinidad is mentioned as a fighter the first thing that comes to your mind is how hard he hits?

Fighters whose styles are not based on going through their opponents can change and ultimately have a Plan B. They are the boxers, not the swarmers and sluggers. Sugar Ray Leonard in his first fight with Roberto Duran was lured into a flatfooted toe-to-toe style fight. This nullified Leonard's speed and boxing ability and played right into Duran's style. This resulted in Leonard enduring more punishment than in any previous fight, causing him to suffer his first defeat. In the rematch five months later, Leonard fought his fight—using the ring and giving Duran angles and keeping the fight in ring center. He never got caught in the corner or with his back against the ropes. This frustrated Duran and led him to say, "No Mas," enabling Leonard to regain the welterweight title.

Some fighters who need to adjust their style for a certain opponent can't because they are swarming pressure fighters who are only effective moving forward. When they inevitably face that opponent who they either can't catch or who can take their punch, they are basically rendered ineffective. These are the fighters for whom Plan B does not exist. The swarmer or the puncher cannot become a boxer. Once he is forced to taper his aggression to try and win, he has no chance.

An example would be Joe Frazier's two fights with George Foreman. Frazier lost his undisputed Heavyweight Title to Foreman via a second round TKO in their first fight. In that fight he came out "smokin," bringing the fight to Foreman like he had in his previous 29 fights where he never tasted defeat. Carrying the fight to Foreman didn't work since Foreman was the bigger puncher, and Joe went right into Foreman's power zone, which cost him the title. When they fought a second time, Joe tried to resort to a Plan B. Instead of pressing the fight he moved away from Foreman and tried to elude his powerful punches. All this did was prolong the inevitable. Instead of getting stopped in two rounds, it lasted five before Joe was TKO'd. When Joe moved away and tried to box instead of fight, he nullified his own fierce punching power, changing his style for one opponent. Frazier was a fish out of water trying to box the taller and longer Foreman. There is no such thing as a Plan B for a Joe Frazier. How about Frazier's nemesis George Foreman? When Foreman defended the title he took from Joe against Ali, he fought with his typical aggressive rage.

Foreman had employed the same style on his way to a 40-0 record, only this time he met an opponent who could take his punch. Foreman punched himself out trying to knock out Ali, but the result was Ali scoring an eighth round knockout, and becoming only the second fighter to regain the undisputed Heavyweight Championship. Foreman, in trying to prepare for a rematch with Ali, fought Jimmy Young who was a crafty boxer, hoping to be better prepared for Ali's style. This resulted in Foreman trying to pace himself against Young. He performed poorly, attempting to be a boxer and basically throwing away his God-given-devastating punch. By Foreman trying to go to Plan B, he lost a decision to a fighter who should never have been in a position to defeat him. If Foreman had fought Young like he did Ali, he would have stopped Young inside of four rounds because Young could not stand up to the fierce assault that Ali had. There is no such thing as a Plan B for a George Foreman.

Looking back at history's greatest fighters, it is impossible not to see that an overwhelming majority are the fighters who possessed the ability to change their styles for a certain opponent. Think about the names that embody that list: Robinson, the Leonards, Ray and Benny, Ali, Holmes, Moore, Holyfield, Hearns, Monzon, Hagler and too many others to mention in this space. What do these fighters share? They all have the ability to adapt to certain opponents as needed to win the fight, especially if a particular fighter's style presents difficulties for them.

In boxing, like most other sports, A+B doesn't always equal C. Greatness is defined by being able to come up with answers to the problems presented by some awkward or unorthodox fighters whose style negates what they are most comfortable with or what they do best. They can adjust and turn the fight back with them in control. The important thing to remember is that Plan B cannot be a blanket statement. One size doesn't fit all.

Rating Fighters Past and Present: Pointless Until Career Complete

By Frank J. Lotierzo
Published, March issue, Wail Cyberboxing zone.com

Can we as boxing columnists please stop matching the Champions of today with past greats? It's just my opinion but a present day title-holder cannot be fairly or accurately ranked until his career is completed. No one can predict how a supposedly great champion of today, undefeated or not, is going to rank until his career has heard its last bell.

Case in point: As recently as 21 months ago a well-respected monthly boxing publication matched Oscar De la Hoya against 10 of the greatest welterweight champions ever. In the panel's opinion, the then undefeated De La Hoya would have defeated all but three of their top 10, which included Sugar Ray Leonard and Thomas Hearns.

I say to them, based on what?

After seeing former lightweight champion Shane Mosley out-box and out-punch De la Hoya in only his third fight as a Welterweight, I wonder how the same panel would rank the slightly—tarnished "Golden Boy". Could they possibly have believed that on his best day he would have beaten Sugar Ray or the "Hit Man"? I question whether Oscar could have beaten the best Donald Curry or Wilfred Benitez. And it's not a given that he could beat Carlos Palomino.

Did you know that in 1968 "Mr Boxing," Nat Fleisher, the founder of Ring magazine, did not have Muhammad Ali ranked in his top ten heavyweights of all time? However, his top 10 did include the likes of Jim Jeffries, Max Schmeling and James Braddock. I believe it is reasonable to assume that had Fleischer lived to see Ali's entire career, he would have been capable of making a more balanced evaluation, "Mr.Boxing" questioned Ali's toughness and ability to take a punch from a proven knockout puncher. Had he been around to see Ali's three fights with Joe Frazier and his title-winning effort against the fearsome George Foreman, Fleischer would have seen that Jeffries, Schmeling and Braddock had nothing to beat Ali with. He would painfully have had to admit that all three of them would have been only too glad to pay their way into a gym just to see Ali hit the heavy bag.

Still not convinced? Here's the best example for waiting until a fighter's career has ended before evaluating his place among the all-time greats: In 1988 another high-profile boxing publication rated then-undefeated heavyweight champion Mike Tyson the second-greatest heavyweight ever. Only the incomparable Muhammad Ali ranked above him. Incidentally, this ranking came on the heels of Tyson's 91-second knockout of 31-year—old former light heavyweight champion Michael Spinks. Does knocking out an over-fed 175-pounder in the signature fight of his career afford such a lofty place in history? Not when 21months later, Tyson was seen searching the canvas for his mouthpiece while being counted out against a journeyman named Buster Douglas-the same Buster Douglas who had been KO'd in three of four career defeats and entered the ring against Tyson in Tokyo a 42-1 underdog. Douglas will be remembered forever for being the first fighter to expose the myth called Mike Tyson. He also provided answers to the questions that some of us had about Tyson.

What kind of chin does he have; can he get up off the canvas to win a fight; and how will he cope with a fighter who can take his punch?

Six years later, Evander Holyfield, coming off the two worst fights of his career (the third bout with Riddick Bowe, in which he was knocked out, and a desultory effort against Bobby Czyz) showed, in front of the largest viewing audience ever to witness a televised fight, undeniable proof of Tyson's shortcomings. Holyfield, who had to be medically cleared to fight by the Mayo Clinic, erased any benefit of doubt afforded Tyson after the Douglas fight by scoring a Round 11 TKO. Once again Tyson showed he could not cope with a fighter who refused to be intimidated and even dared to fight back. In the rematch eight months later Tyson showed he could not take a "butt-kicking" like a champion. When Tyson committed the most cowardly act in boxing history by biting both of Holyfield's ears, he was telling us that he wanted out of the fight before he was knocked out by Holyfield for the second consecutive time.

Is this the body of work of a fighter considered to be the second-best heavyweight ever by some of those who are supposed to know? They could not have been more wrong! A fighter's career must be complete in order to determine when he was truly at his best. Trying to match yesterday's fighters with those of today is about as credible as the computer that said light heavyweight champion Bob Foster would knock out heavyweight champion Joe Frazier one month before they fought. Frazier went on to knock Foster out cold in the second round.

Dempsey and Tunney: The making of Legends

By Tom Donelson

Jess Willard stepped into the ring on July 4th to defend his heavy-weight championship-his first fight in three years. Willard, with a 60 pound and 5 inch height advantage over his opponent, was confident that this fight would be short and sweet. An impressive giant, Willard lived off one fight-his victory over Jack Johnson four years earlier. He was the "Great White Hope" that succeeded.

Willard's notoriety was built around one fight and as the late boxing historian Nat Fleischer wrote, "It is quite a paradox that Willard, one of the poorest of the heavyweight champions, should have taken the crown from one of the greatest." Jack Johnson dominated most of the fight, cutting up Willard's face, but Willard's strength finally caught up with the older fighter. Willard ended the fight in the 26th round with a right to the jaw and his fame ensured. Now four years later, Willard is ready to collect another payday for his fight with Jack Dempsey worth $100,000-a huge sum in those days. The July 4th match would provide Willard with his biggest purse and his worst defeat.

Willard looked at Dempsey as a little boy and considered the fight a joke. Willard told Grantland Rice, "He'll come tearing into me. I will have my left out. Then I will hit him with a right uppercut. That'll be the end." The disparity between the two fighters could not be more obvious as they both stepped in the ring. Willard's body was pale white; Dempsey's body was tanned and sculptured. Dempsey looked like a fighter in spite of the height and weight difference. Jack Dempsey's ferocity overcame the height and weight advantage of his opponent.

The first round of the fight would be a transitional round between the old and new. Willard fought straight up with his hands low. Depending upon his size advantage, Willard plodded slowly forward. Dempsey resembled a Tiger chasing an ox. Looking more like a modern fighter with hands up high, Dempsey used his superior boxing skills and quickness to move under the slower Willard's jab. After the first few moments, Dempsey ducked under a Willard jab to smack a hard right to the body and landed a devastating hook to Willard's face. Willard's cheek caved in and down went the giant fighter. This was the first of seven knockdowns. In 1919, a boxer did not have to go to the neutral corner after a knock-down and a fighter could begin his attack as soon as his opponent's knee left the canvas.

Dempsey stayed within punching range as the referee began his count. As soon as Willard's knee left the canvas, Dempsey pummeled him with lethal combinations of lefts and rights. This pattern repeated itself six more times as Dempsey beat Willard senseless as Willard attempted to get up. Dempsey unleashed barrages of lefts and rights upon the helpless Willard. As the bell sounded, Willard's butt was on the canvas as his corner rescued him.

Dempsey, thinking the fight was over, actually left the corner and when Willard got back up to start the second round, Dempsey had to be called back. Dempsey continued his onslaught, as Willard became a human punching bag. After the third round, Willard's body gave out. One side of the champion's face was swollen twice its size and his cheek was fractured. With his eyes closed and blood spurting from his nose; Willard could barely leave the ring due to broken ribs and labored breathing. A new legend was born.

Dempsey's rise to the heavyweight championship began in the West beginning his career as a club fighter. United with Doc Kearns as his manager, Dempsey began his climb to the top. He lived the life of a hobo as a young man, a life that included a marriage to a prostitute and fighting off other men's advances on boxcars. The young Dempsey's life evolved from a tough America where fighting was a way of life and Dempsey became very good at it.

The devastation of Willard set in motion Dempsey's legend. This fight promoted by Tex Rickard was the first of many mega fights that featured Dempsey with his punching power aiding his drawing power. Dempsey was not universally loved due to avoiding military service in the First World War, but he would become one of the most recognized sport athletes in the 1920's. As sporting events grew in popularity, Boxing rode on Jack Dempsey's shoulder. When Dempsey retired in 1928, million dollar gates became a new standard for boxing receipts. The real impact of Dempsey as well as his major rival, Gene Tunney, was his impact on boxing's style. He fought with relentless desire, bobbing and weaving before striking an opponent. He kept his hands up high and his boxing skills resemble modern day fighters. Before Dempsey, fights would be scheduled for as many as 45 rounds with fighters tending to conserve their energy until later rounds. With the advent of Dempsey, championship fights became a standard 15 rounds. This meant that a fighter could fight more aggressively and trained in a more logical manner. Dempsey would fight every minute and there was no conserving energy against the constant forward movement of Dempsey.

Roger Kahn observed that, "From Dempsey's day onward boxers have been trained so they develop the strength, stamina and wind to go fifteen rounds. Given the fifteen round limit, there are reasonably precise formulae for how many miles a boxer in serious training should run every day, and how many rounds he should spar each afternoon." Dempsey's regimen included six-mile runs, sparring, shadowboxing, hitting bags and skipping rope in selected intervals. Dempsey initiated the modern boxing training method. His superior conditioning allowed him to overpower the larger Willard.

Grantland Rice described Dempsey's boxing style as "a method of weaving and moving about that was partly defense but it always led to attack or headlong assault...Dempsey was not a bad boxer...he was none too easy to hit with a good punch." Dempsey was not the boxer that Tunney was, but he did have basic skills that complimented his offensive style. In his fight with Willard, Dempsey avoided Willard's heavy punches and developed his own power punches to claim the World Championship.

As the decade of the 20's opened, Dempsey would be one of the decades leading stars along with Babe Ruth and Tennis star Bill Tilden. Dempsey was part of a decade where heroes strode the sports world as legendary gods celebrated for their deeds. Sports writers such as Grantland Rice wrote poetry, celebrating their heroes' exploits similar to ancient Greek writers describing their heroes of yore.

> *Ty and the Big Babe, Matty and Cy,*
> *Dempsey and Tunney—Thorpe and the rest—*
> *Where are the mighty who held the road?*
> *Those who dwelt in the gods' abode?*
> *Where are the kings who ruled the play?*
> *Over the hills and far away*
> *Over the hills and far away.*
> *Grantland Rice*

Gene Tunney was Captain Ahab in search of Moby Dick. Moby Dick in this case being Jack Dempsey. Tunney captured the United States light heavyweight championship in 1922 and dominated this division before moving up to the Heavyweight division. The former Marine prepared for his eventual match with Dempsey by studying the champion's style. When noted sports writer Grantland Rice first met Tunney in 1921, Tunney stunned him with the declaration, "Dempsey is the one I want." Rice, like others, never conceived that Tunney would ever beat the great Jack Dempsey. As a master boxer, Tunney understood that he had the perfect style to counter the more dynamic and crushing style of Dempsey. In 1925, Tunney began his campaign for the heavyweight championship by knocking out Tom Gibbons, who just two years earlier went the distance with Jack Dempsey. For

Tunney, his fight with Dempsey would define his greatness. To be the best, you had to beat the best. It was not a quest of hatred, but a mountain to be climbed.

On September 23rd, 1926, Tunney walked into the ring as the challenger and walked out as champion, his years of studies justified. At the age of 31, Jack Dempsey was not the fighter of old and Tunney took advantage of Dempsey's ring rust by easily dancing around the slower Dempsey. Dempsey could not recapture the magic of yesteryear and overcome three years of inactivity. Dempsey's eyes were nearly closed and his face puffed up at the end of the fight. At the end of the fight, Dempsey asked one of his seconds, "to take me to him (Tunney)…I want to shake his hand." Dempsey could not even see his conqueror after the first fight.

Dempsey showed class in acknowledging his defeat and Americans finally accepted Dempsey as one of their own. Boxing is one sport in which nobility in defeat brings honor and fight fans often admire a fighter who comes back from defeat as opposed to loving a fighter who wins in easy fashion. Dempsey went back into training as he prepared for an elimination fight with Jack Sharkey. Behind on points, Dempsey nailed Sharkey with a tough body shot that Sharkey thought too low. As Sharkey complained to the referee, Dempsey finished Sharkey with a left hook. Sharkey forgot the golden rule of boxing-always protect yourself. Dempsey prepared for his second shot at Tunney.

The second fight, taking place in Chicago, was the biggest fight in boxing history. All of America was listening to their radios as they heard Tunney easily dominate the first six rounds, with Tunney's speed and boxing skill proving too much for the plodding Dempsey. The seventh round would provide Boxing with one of its biggest controversies and dramatic moments. As the round began, a desperate Dempsey attacked Tunney with one last charge. For one brief moment, the Dempsey of old appeared. He battered Tunney with a series of blows, with a right hand jab finishing the job as Tunney dropped to the canvas. Before the fight, both fighters agreed to a new rule that the other fighter would proceed to the neutral corner after a knockdown. Dempsey stood over Tunney, waiting to finish the job. The referee refused to start counting until Dempsey moved to the neutral corner. This gave Tunney an extra four-five seconds to recover. Tunney listened to the count getting up at the count of nine. Tunney moved and danced as Dempsey stalked his prey, unable to finish the job. A desperate Dempsey pleaded with Tunney to stand and fight. Tunney kept moving and ducking frantic bombs thrown by Dempsey. Dempsey's punches did not find their target and Tunney survived the round.

Tunney, in the very next round, returned the favor by knocking down Dempsey and then pummeled a tired Dempsey for the rest of the fight. Most boxing historians remembered the seventh round and the long count. They forget that Tunney mastered Dempsey for most of the 20 rounds that these two men fought. While many viewed Dempsey as an old fighter, the reality is that Dempsey's conditioning was due to his lack of training over the previous three-year period before the Tunney fight. At the age of 32, he was a victim of his good life. Tunney, Dempsey's junior by three years, proved to be in better shape and this allowed him to win.

Questions do remain about the fight. Dave Barry, the referee, owned a speakeasy and had mob connections. Philadelphia mobster Boo Boo Hoff and gambler Abe Attell loaned Tunney $200,000. (On the other hand, Al Capone was a big fan of Jack Dempsey. Both fighters had supporters among the many factions of organized crime.) While most Americans remained ignorant of the growing mobster control of boxing, Barry's own connection certainly effected his refereeing. Barry's delay in beginning the count could easily be connected to his own underworld connections and this delay certainly aided in Tunney recovering from Dempsey's blow. We will never know if Tunney could get up and execute his retreat if the count started sooner. When Dempsey hit the ground in the next round, Barry began the count immediately and never asked Tunney to move to a neutral corner. In the first quarter century, gambling and sports fixing remained serious problems, more so than today. In 1919, the Chicago White Sox threw the World Series and even during the 1920's, rumors of baseball games being fixed still persisted. Boxing was not immune to the lure of the mob but this fight was the beginning of extensive mob interest in the fight game. The Mob's control of boxing remained until the early 60's.

The new rule of having a fighter going to a neutral corner after a knockdown gave boxers a chance to recover and hurt fighters like Dempsey, who hovered over their opponents. As Tunney showed, an extra 4-5 seconds can be the difference in winning a fight or losing it. Very rarely do Heavyweight fights match two great fighters, close to their peak but this fight did exactly that. Dempsey and Tunney dominated the heavyweight division throughout the 20's. We would not see a similar match until the Frazier-Ali bout in 1971.

Tunney and Dempsey were symbolic of their era and as fighters, they attracted the attention of the boxing public. Their fights went the distance and provided the last closing act to "the golden age of sports" before the big economic crash that loomed over the horizon. After Tunney retired in 1928, mediocrity dominated Boxing until Joe Louis began his reign as champion in1937. Tunney-Dempsey was a holy war of nobility between two great fighters, whose class transcended the ring. What this fight proved in the end was that Tunney was the better boxer.

Many observers, even today, feel Dempsey's loss was due to his age. Boxing reporter James Doyle reflected the opinion then and now when he wrote, "Dempsey was a beaten man, it seemed to me, from the moment he entered the ring. To say he was a mere shell of the Dempsey of other years, would be obvious. He was, in truth, hardly a shell of the Dempsey of old." It is true that Jack Dempsey did not fight for three years, but Jack Dempsey chose not to fight in those intervening years. In 1926, Dempsey was only 31 years old, certainly not over the hill. Sugar Ray Robinson and Sugar Ray Leonard came back successfully after a similar lay-off against top-ranked competitors. In 1926, another 31 year old was dominating the sport of Baseball, and in the following year he would set the home run record that stood for 33 years. That man was George Herman Ruth, a man whose nightlife adventures would rival any man.

Former heavyweight champion James J. Corbett summed up Tunney's advantages by noting, "The victory of Gene Tunney tonight over Jack Dempsey again demonstrated the superiority of the boxer over a slugger. It was Tunney in perfect fighting condition, as opposed to Dempsey in the pink, the master boxer against the super slugger—and Tunney won. But in this crisis of Tunney's reign as the king of pugilism, his boxing skill, his generalship and his keen ring brain thwarted the slugger and the boxer remains at the pinnacle of pugilism."

Tunney's fighting style was ahead of his time. One boxing historian observed, "Gene Tunney—Perhaps the most underrated fighter in the history of boxing. Tunney was the ultimate stylist—slick but tough as nails, who along with fellow champion, lightweight immortal & contemporary, Benny Leonard, introduced the modern era of boxing as we know it today... This was evidenced some 40 plus years later, when a young Cassius Clay adapted many of Tunney's slick moves into his own unique arsenal." In both fights, Tunney dominated Dempsey. James Doyle's account of the first fight easily resembled the second fight when he wrote," During his leather-mitted reply to the now confounded critics who said he'd have never a chance with the scowling Manassan, Gene Tunney whipped Jack Dempsey through virtually every minute of ten surprising rounds." With the exception of the 7th round, Tunney easily won the fight. By the end of the second fight, Dempsey was reeling and ready to be knocked out. Only his courage kept him standing as Shirley Povich surveyed, "He was beaten thoroughly in a bout that was tame for a championship bout—in a bout that saw a mechanically great fighter reach down in his heart and find the courage to go on and beat a man who had not the stamina nor physical ability to match the Spartan courage that has never been disputed."

The real controversy is whether Tunney could have survived the 7th round if there was no long count. Dr. Feddie Pacheco says no. "I have to conclude that if the injured Gene Tunney had gotten up at a legitimate eight count, he would clearly have been knocked out" says the fight Doctor. Boxing historian Alex Hall disagreed. Mr. Hall countered, "Dempsey himself claimed that he did not agree with the notion that his foul tactics had cost him the victory. Tunney does appear dazed at first but can clearly be seen to be ready for action before ten seconds (official or not) had elapsed."

Dempsey had trouble with boxers and Tunney was the best boxer of his era. Would Dempsey have beaten Tunney, if he had been in shape or if he was the Dempsey of three years earlier? Alex Hall also recorded that Dempsey had trouble with a smaller but quicker Tom Gibbons three years earlier. Using his speed, Gibbons survived Dempsey's onslaught for 15 rounds and went the distance. Gibbons was not in Tunney's class as a boxer. Dempsey was a fierce competitor and hard puncher, who would have been competitive in any era. It is debatable to suggest that Dempsey in his prime would have defeated Tunney.

Over 20 rounds Tunney dominated Dempsey easily. On the eve of their second fight, Dempsey was in top shape and had won a preliminary fight against Sharkey. Tunney on the other hand, did not fight for a full year after his first fight. The results were the same as the year before-Tunney beat Dempsey.

After the fight, Dempsey became an American hero. He started a successful restaurant on Broadway and joined the armed forces during World War II, wiping out the memories of his World War I avoidance of combat. He even served in the Pacific arena during the tail end of World War II, landing on Okinawa. These fights legitimatize Dempsey in a way that his victories never did with America falling in love with Dempsey. A Dempsey cult developed about the fighter, often exaggerating his accomplishments.

Tunney quit on top. After fighting Dempsey, he knocked out Tom Heeney and then retired. He invested his money well, and well into his

50's he sat on Corporate boards. His son even became a United States Senator from California. Both men joined the folklore of boxing history and this fight sealed their place as two of boxing's greatest. Tunney's greatness came from his singled-minded pursuit of Dempsey whereas Dempsey's nobility in defeat endeared him to the American public. This fight was the biggest grossing live gate at the time and it would take another 50 years before this record was broken. Both men found economic security as they got older—a luxury rarely accorded most boxers. As memories dim of those two fights, only legend is left.

What memories we have are a few reels and the written word. Oral history dominates our memories of these fighters and what we are left with is the imagination of Dempsey's right hand crashing over Tunney's left eye in the famous seventh round. These two giants became larger in our memory as time faded and the last remaining witness of this fight drifted to the Holy Father in heaven. This fight represented the end of a more innocent time where sports writers wrote legendary prose about larger than life warriors carving one another with jabs and crosses

Lotierzo on the Tunney-Dempsey rivalry
(Frank Lotierzo adds a few notes to the Tunney-Dempsey rivalry)

Most boxing observers forget Tunney had Dempsey down in the eighth round and that he beat Dempsey 19 out of 20 rounds. Harry Greb fought Tunney five times and he sparred with Dempsey, who sparred like he fought. When the press asked Greb whom he was picking to win before their first fight, Greb told them, "if you're picking Dempsey, you are wrong." He continued, "If you want to make yourself look smart, pick Tunney to win. I know what I'm talking about. I was in the ring with both and I am telling you, Tunney is the better fighter."

I watched the replay of the long count many times. I feel Tunney could've risen when Barry counted nine, Tunney was so smart that he took advantage of the extra seconds he had. While he was down, he was looking at Barry and seemed to have the sense to get up at nine. In those days, the Champion could pick the distance of the fight. Dempsey chose the fight to be ten rounds because he was coming off a long hiatus between fights.

Here is a dream fight. How about Tunney vs Marciano? I believe that Marciano probably wins, but it wouldn't be a walkover. Sugar Ray Leonard did the same as Tunney in preparing for Marvelous Marvin Hagler. Leonard studied Hagler for three years before they fought. Leonard never stopped training while he was retired. After watching Hagler fight Duran, Leonard saw Hagler being caught by Duran's right. After seeing this, Leonard felt that was something he could take advantage of. And he did.

Frank Lotierzo on Louis-Marciano

(An answer to a friend's EMAIL dealing with a question on what would happen if Marciano, Joe Frazier and George Foreman fought Louis in his prime.)

When Louis fought Marciano, Louis was a shell of what he was in his prime. Louis took Marciano's best shots for eight rounds and had nothing to return. Louis in his prime, would have nailed Rocky coming in. Louis was the best ever at drawing his opponents to him. I believe that Louis was the most dangerous when fighters went straight at him. I believe that Marciano, Joe Frazier and George Foreman would have played right into his net. Of the three, Foreman would have the best shot at beating Louis because of his size and strength.

In my opinion, Louis is the best fundamental fighter in any weight class. I have studied Louis in depth and have seen fifteen of his fights. Joe Louis was vulnerable to movers whereas Marciano, Frazier and Foreman go right to you. This is suicide against Louis. If you watch Louis closely, he moves ever so slightly forward, but that is to draw you in. Frazier, Foreman and Marciano would all go to Louis and be in line for his devastating right hand. He got if off extremely fast. You could also make a case that Louis didn't have as good a chin as these three individuals, since he hit the deck seven times in his career.

Savarese's Last Stand

By Frank Lotierzo

Editor's note: This was written before Lou Savarese was to fight Mike Tyson, a fight that Savarese would lose.

The day that Lou Savarese fought Mike Tyson would represent his last chance to have any say in the Heavyweight division. Despite a record of 39-3 with 32 knock outs since turning pro, the former New York Golden Gloves Heavyweight Champion had never fought for a world title. The only title that the 6' 5" Savarese won was the Regional U.S. Boxing Association title, where he TKO'd Buster Mathis Jr. in the 7th round on November 1, 1996.

The win over Mathis propelled Savarese into a big money high profile bout with George Foreman shown on HBO. Although Savarese lost a split decision, he fought with more determination and boxing savvy than he had previously shown. Six months later, highly touted David Izon stopped Savarese after being knocked down twice in the 5th round, the only time Savarese has ever been stopped. After suffering back-to-back defeats in 1997, he scored two consecutive knockouts in 1998. The second was over Mike Tyson's conqueror Buster Douglas, who was in the midst of a successful comeback after recovering from a diabetic coma. A Tyson-Douglas rematch hinged on a Douglas victory. Because of the devastating defeat suffered by Douglas, those plans were scrapped.

Savarese split his next two fights, winning a tough decision over up and coming Lance "Mount" Whitaker. (Whitaker's new nickname is Goofi.) Surviving an 8th round knockdown, Savarese rallied in rounds

9th and 10th to secure the decision. In his last fight before Tyson, he was convincingly beaten by then number one rated Michael Grant, as seen before, Savarese's huge heart helped him survive two 10th round knockdowns and hold on only to hear the unanimous decision announced in favor of Grant.

Twelve months after losing to Grant, Savarese faced former Heavyweight Champ Mike Tyson. Tyson was ready to repay Savarese for costing him his chance at redemption against Buster Douglas, the fighter who exposed and destroyed his myth. For Savarese, a win could lead to an elusive title shot that he has so desperately pursued. Savarese was chosen because of obvious faults in his game. He was big and easy to hit and he did not have one punch knockout power. In addition, he had not fought in a year. Savarese did not know the meaning of fear or quit, an important character trait when fighting Tyson. At 34, Savarese was aware that he could not let this opportunity slip.

His strategy was to make Tyson respect him before the end of the first round and he had to utilize his reach to keep Tyson in the center of the ring to set up his right hand. He had to tie Tyson up on the inside and try to extend the fight into the second half where Tyson became vulnerable to the right uppercut. Savarese was ready to retaliate against any foul delivered by Tyson or Tyson would continue to foul throughout the fight. This was Savarese's strategy.

Savarese walked into the ring, ready for the fight of his life. Then, within the first round, the dream was over. All his preparation went for naught as he found himself knocked out. For Savarese, this fight represented the dividing line between legitimate heavyweight contender to mere opponent. After the fight, Lou Savarese was merely an opponent.

James Page and "Six Heads" Lewis

By Frank Lotierzo

Editor's note: These are Frank Lotierzo's reflections upon James Page before he lost his title to "Six Heads" Lewis.

Since turning pro in 1990, WBA Welterweight Champion James Page (25-3) had done everything asked of a fighter. The problem was that the former back to back national Golden Gloves silver medallist was that he fought in the weight class as Shane Mosely and Oscar De Hoya. To escape their shadows, he had to get by the hard punching southpaw Andrew "Six Heads" Lewis, who was unbeaten as a pro. A tremendous puncher in his own right, he was prepared for a tough fight. A win here and big payday against either Mosley or De la Hoya was just around the corner.

Page won his title by knocking Andrei Pestriaey with a one-punch knockout. He then defended his title against the hard punching Jose Luis Lopez. Page started off quickly by throwing roundhouse rights and his thunderous left hook. Lopez, who had one of the best chins in boxing, withstood the assault. Midway through the third round, Lopez landed a punishing uppercut, which had Page stumbling all over the ring. Page weathered a vicious two-handed assault by Lopez and was saved by the bell from going down in both round three and four. Beginning in round five, Page began to wear down Lopez with his punishing power. He won a unanimous decision in what turned out to the fight of the year. Afterward, the cocky Lopez, who had refused to acknowledge Page as the real champion, was humble and gracious in defeat.

Page defended his title two more times. Going into the Lewis fight, Page had an eight fight unbeaten streak with six of those wins coming by knockout. His opponent may have been the best-kept secret in boxing. Andrew Lewis, a native of Guyana, had been a fighter since he was six years old. Lewis came into this bout unbeaten and his trainer described him as a fighter "who threw 130 punches per round." A resourceful boxer, Lewis possessed a tremendous jab. For Lewis, this fight was his big chance at the big time. Lewis wanted to be first man from Guyana to win a boxing championship and many top contenders avoided "Six Heads."

"Six Heads" nickname came when his first opponent said that was what he saw after being hit by Lewis. And Page must have felt the same way as Lewis went on to win the fight by a knockout. Dominating the fight with a wicked jab followed by crosses and hooks, Lewis slugged his way to the championship. For Page, this defeat meant going back to contender status. For Lewis, the future was bright with chances for bigger paydays and HBO appearances. One fight can determine the future of a fighter. Sometimes, boxers never get a second chance, especially, if they have the potential to knock out opponents. Page's campaign for another championship effectively ended, as he was one fighter that very few boxers wanted any part off.

Rating the Heavy Weights

By Tom Donelson and Frank Lotierzo

It is difficult to rank heavyweights but we are attempting, nonetheless. We based our decision on which boxers we felt would most likely win in a confrontation, as well as their accomplishments within the ring. To be fair, we decided to split our designation between two eras. Until 1928 boxers were not required to go to a neutral corner, and it was not until the 1920's that championship fights were consistently 15 rounds or less.

Going to the neutral corner changed the dynamics of the fight game. For example, when Dempsey destroyed Jess Willard, he stayed within arms length of Willard. The moment that Willard lifted his knee off the canvas, Dempsey rained more punches upon the helpless Willard. Willard never had a chance after the first knockdown. Forcing a fighter to go to a neutral corner, gave a boxer an extra 2-3 seconds to survive and move out of harms way.

Roger Kahn observed that moving championship bouts to 15 rounds changed strategy and training. Future boxers "trained so that they developed the strength, stamina and wind to go fifteen rounds. Given the fifteen round limit, there are reasonably precise formulae for how many miles a boxer in serious training should run every day and how many rounds he should spar each afternoon." Dempsey's regimen included six-mile runs, sparring, shadowboxing, hitting bags and skipping rope in selected intervals. Dempsey began the modern boxing training method. His superior conditioning allowed him to overpower the larger Willard and survive the Firpo fight in 1923.

We rate the top 10 boxers from 1930 on and due to changes in rules and in fairness to the early boxers, we ranked the top heavyweight champions before 1930. Gene Tunney and Jack Dempsey were included in the older generation even though they were the first to fight with the neutral corner rule in their second match. They spent most of their careers fighting under different rules than many of their early contemporaries.

We only rank champions, but concede that many good fighters such as Sam Langford and Harry Wills were denied a chance at the championship due to the color of their skin.

Ali was the greatest based on two factors, his ability to endure punishment and his ability to adapt to any given situation. He dominated in an era that was filled with great heavyweights. Liston, Foreman and Frazier all were top ten heavyweights and no fighter had ever beaten this caliber of fighters before Ali. His speed and underestimated power would have allowed him to stand with any fighter of any era.

Ali's body strength and his ability to take a punch is what allowed him to beat Frazier and Foreman. It was not his hand or his mobility. Let's face it, Ali did not show any foot movement against Foreman, but he showed his quick hands and ability to take punches. Ali possessed a cast iron chin complemented by a concrete body. These were weapons that boxing experts and fans couldn't see and didn't suspect until he was tested by Smokin' Joe Frazier and George Foreman. When Ali tied up Frazier, Foreman and Liston, he kept them from doing anything and waited until the ref broke them up. If Ali had just a little less strength or chin, he would have lost all three fights to Frazier. He would not have survived to fight another day.

Ali had the ability and skin to adapt to any situation. His rope-a-dope against Foreman was just one example. Ali realized that he could not dance and move for 15 rounds and survive, so he changed tactics. Ali outsmarted Foreman. It is these intangibles that lead us to conclude that Ali was the greatest. His hand speed, his body strength, and underestimated punching power would allow him to survive Joe Louis. Louis was a great fighter and the most technically sound fighter in the heavyweight division. Ali, on the other hand, was an unorthodox fighter whose speed allowed him to do pretty much what he wanted, and that is why he would have triumphed over Joe Louis.

Joe Louis' record speaks for itself. For 12 years, Louis was the king of the heavyweights, fighting cute boxers such as Conn and chopping down giants such as Abe Simon and Buddy Baer. His sound technical skills provided a clinic for heavyweight boxers of the future and his ability to cut off the ring allowed him to deal with the quicker fighters. As he said about Billy Conn, "he can run but he can not hide." His quick hands and power allowed him to finish off any opponent. While we feel that Ali's overall skills would allow the "Greatest" to prevail over Louis, you could make the case in favor of Louis.

One question that came up when we researched our list of the greatest fighters—would Joe Louis have beaten Rocky Marciano in his prime? Joe Louis was a shell of himself when he fought Marciano. Louis took Rocky's best shots for eight rounds but could not deliver in return. His body could no longer do what his mind commanded. In Louis' prime, he would have nailed Rocky as Rocky was coming in. Louis loved it when fighters came to him, and was the best at drawing opponents to him. Marciano, Frazier and Foreman would have fought in front of Louis. Of these three, Foreman would have the best chance to beat Louis.

When we reviewed several of Louis' fights, we found that Louis was the best fundamentally sound fighter in any weight class. He had good techniques and when he had his opponent in trouble, it was over. Louis had a devastating right hand combined with a sharp jab-a lethal combination.

These two fighters were head and shoulders above all fighters since 1930, but other fighters on our list demonstrated their own greatness in their time. Liston and Foreman were two of the hardest punchers, whose reputations were stained by losing to Ali. Before Liston met Ali, he was the baddest man in the Heavyweight universe. Liston cleaned out the leading heavyweight contenders before he became champion, fighting the good fighters whom Patterson ducked. When Liston met Patterson, it only confirmed what was already known—Liston was the best. At least until he met Ali!

Liston would have beaten either Frazier or Marciano. Both fighters would have gone directly to Liston just as he trained for, and was best at. Ali was too fast in their first fight. Some stated that Liston was past his prime when he fought Ali but others disagreed, pointing out that Liston was the heavy favorite when he entered the Ali fight. Liston demolished everybody but Eddie Machen, who came closer than any-one other than Ali to beating Liston. (Machen spent the entire fight running and merely wanted to survive.) Cleveland Williams fought Liston because he was a big puncher, but only lasted 2 rounds in their first fight and 3 in their second fight. Liston lost to Leotis Martin but was a shot fighter by the time they fought. His connection with orga-nized crime, and Cus D' Amato's ability to protect Patterson from legitimate competition prevented Liston from having a chance at the championship belt earlier.

When you look at Liston's career closer, it becomes even more impressive. Before Ali, boxing experts were saying that Liston was even better than Louis. Between 1958 and 1962, Liston won 21 fights with 18 knockouts. Cus D' Amato knew that if his fighter fought Liston, he would lose. Liston's reputation collapsed with his two losses to Ali. It was the way he lost that diminished Liston's reputation. He ended the first fight by sitting on his stool, and in the second fight simply went down after getting hit with a right hand. Against boxers just as Larry Holmes and Lennox Lewis, he would have been like Joe Frazier, attacking. At 6-2", he was bigger than Frazier or Tyson but would have swarmed his opponent in a similar style. The more one looks at Liston, the better he looks. If you take out Leotis Martin and the Ali fight, he won 50 out of 51 fights with 39 knockouts. His loss to Marty Marshall occurred in his ninth fight and avenged that loss.

We considered Liston the fourth best heavyweight behind George Foreman. Ali's defeat of both fighters simply adds to Ali's greatness.

Foreman was the hardest punching heavyweight champion and while Ali overshadowed Foreman, Foreman showed his overall heart and skill when he recaptured the title 21 years after he lost it to Ali!

Frazier and Marciano were those swarmers who dominated boxers. Marciano retired undefeated, but the quality of his opponents was inferior to those of Frazier's. Marciano would not have retired undefeated had he fought in the 60's or the 70's. Like other fighters of his era, Ali overshadowed Frazier, but Frazier did beat Ali in the fight of the century at the Mecca of boxing, Madison Square Garden. His loss to Foreman diminished his career in the eyes of many fight experts, but Foreman would have beaten either Tyson or Marciano just as easily. It is a case of a smaller heavyweight being swallowed up by a stronger fighter.

Holyfield was the fighter of the 90's but Lewis may yet be given credit for his accomplishments. Lennox Lewis' problem is that he lost to fighters he had no business losing to. Holyfield fought all the best fighters of his era and beat most of them. Tyson's reputation was built upon his early career but losses to Buster Douglas and later to Holyfield and Lewis hurts his standing with boxing historians.

While some would hold his losses to Lewis against him, Holyfield in his fight against Lewis could only fight in spurts. He was not able to fight a whole round like he could against Foreman, Bowe, Mercer and even Tyson. Lewis, despite his wins against Holyfield, could not be ranked higher than Holyfield.

Holyfield fought all the best fighters of his era, winning most of his bouts. While Holyfield had trouble with the tall boxer-puncher, he was still able to win against all styles. Lewis' victory over Holyfield and Tyson may yet convince boxing historians to rank him higher.

As for rating fighters before 1930, it becomes a dicey proposition. Gene Tunney was the best boxer of this era, his foot movement and power allowing him to dominate Dempsey in their two epic fights. This reason alone would qualify Tunney as the best of the pre 1930's era, even though that pits us against boxing experts who hold Dempsey, Jefferies and Johnson in higher regard.

Jack Johnson was the best boxer before the 1920's. Jefferies was the most feared slugger until he retired. Jefferies depended upon brute strength as opposed to Johnson who used defensive parry and counter attacking styles. Johnson was not busy enough to keep Dempsey off him, and we believe that Dempsey would have walked right through him. When Johnson defeated Jefferies, Jefferies had been retired for six years before coming back. While Jefferies lasted 15 rounds, Jack Johnson allowed the older white fighter to survive, so he could torture his outclassed opponent. According to sports writers of his day, Johnson traditionally tortured his opponents before dispatching them. Johnson was strong enough to hold off Jefferies' strength and win. At his peak, Johnson would have beaten Jefferies in our opinion. But, it could have gone the other way according to some of the boxing experts we talked with.

On the other hand, Dempsey would have been busy enough to pressure Johnson and eventually overcome the reluctant Johnson. Johnson could not be circumspect against Dempsey as was his wont.

Gentle Jim Corbett was the first great boxer, using guile and speed to win, though Corbett could not handle the power of either Jefferies or Bob Fitzsimmons (one of the great pound for pound fighters).

Among the early fighters, there were six who stand out. We love Tunney, maybe because he exhibited superior boxing skills and defeated the idol of the 20's, Jack Dempsey. Dempsey may be an overrated fighter but he did pack a powerful punch. When comparing early fighters, it becomes difficult. Jack Johnson spent half of his championship reign running from the authorities for violating the Mann Act and Gentleman Jim Corbett proved to be an excellent boxer with quick feet and hands. Unfortunately, he could not beat the two big bangers of his era, Bob Fitzsimmons and Jim Jefferies. Jefferies was the dominant fighter at the turn of the century and his strength combined with power allowed him to clean out the heavyweight division before retiring. Jefferies would leave retirement six years later to answer the call of the "Great White Hope" and fight Jack Johnson with Johnson humiliating Jefferies in a rout. There are very few films that remain of the early era of boxing, and we have to rely on eyewitness accounts. We picked our list based on our knowledge of these fighters, but are far surer of our picks after the 1930's.

After vigorous debate, we finally agreed upon our list.

All Time Best Fighters

Post-1930's top fighters

Ali
Louis
Foreman
Liston
Frazier
Mariciano
Holmes
Holyfield
Lewis
Tyson

Pre-1930's top fighters
GeneTunney
Jack Dempsey
Jack Johnson
James Jefferies
Bob Fitzsimmons
Gentle Jim Corbett

Addendum: We included interviews and discussion with leading boxing experts to further explore our lists.

Bill Chair of the Philadelphia Inquirer gives his opinion on our selections as part of an interview with Frank Lotierzo:

Frank: Who wins in their prime, Louis or Ali?

Bill: If Louis in his prime had hit Ali with the same left hook as Frazier did, Ali would not have gotten up. And, like Ali, the military cost him the heart of his career.

I saw Marciano dismantle Louis, but Joe was at the very end. I would love to have seen the 1950 Rock vs. the 1940 Louis. But I don't think The Rock could have walked in on Louis, and he didn't have the ring generalship to fight a strategic fight. So styles really make this an impossible list. Louis had the hand speed to hit Ali and was a master at cutting off the ring. He would have walked right through Frazier but would have needed all his game for a man as big as Foreman.

Frank: What was your opinion of Jack Dempsey?

Bill: Dempsey was the Mike Tyson of his time—a vastly overrated puncher who made his reputation by knocking down Willard—a real stiff—a jillion times.

Frank: Who wins between Tyson and Marciano?

Bill: Tyson-Marciano would have been interesting, but I think Rocky's relentless style would have brought out the quit in Tyson and there is plenty of quit there. I've just never been a Holmes man.

Frank: Where do you rank Lennox Lewis?

Bill: I don't think Lewis belongs in this company—he's lost to too many stiffs.

Frank: What fighters impressed you?

Bill: The Jack Johnson I've seen in the old films could have played in this league. He had legit heavyweight size and an unorthodox style. I also think Teofilo Stevenson would have been a great professional if he had defected at around age 20. The man had a very heavy right.

JD Vena of Cyberboxingzone.com gave his opinion and then engaged Frank Lotierzo in a debate on top ten lists.

The Ten Greatest Heavyweights of All Time

By J.D. Vena

One question that continues to linger into the new century is who is the greatest of them all. The age-old question that probably began somewhere in a saloon 100 years ago or so has become more and more difficult for the average pugilistic pundit to answer.

Typically a list of greatest fighters reflects the era in which an individual grew up and other factors that should not have any influence.

Factors such as the impact the fighter had on society or the belief that one fighter's athletic ability was better than another's are just a few of the elements weighed when creating these lists. Some also believe that had fighter A fought in fighter B's era, he would have mopped the floor with his competition. Such speculation will never be proven and therefore cannot be realistically argued. Not many experts today can even predict who would win the contests of today.

Throughout history, the fighters of the present usually do not receive the credit for greatness until those fighters are long retired. For example, in 1950, The Boxing Writer's Association of America took a poll to determine the greatest fighter of the first half of the century. Jack Dempsey received the most votes with over 250. Joe Louis received 130 votes and everyone else received far fewer (including the likes of Sugar Ray Robinson and Henry Armstrong). Why? What did Joe Louis do after 1950 (the year after his 11 ½ year reign ended) that would place him consistently above Dempsey in most of today's boxing writer's top 10 heavyweight lists? Also consider that up until 1950, the great Sugar Ray Robinson lost only one of 105 fights. Certainly Henry Armstrong's achievement of holding 3 titles in 3 different weight classes simultaneously overshadows any of Dempsey's accomplishments as well.

A poll for heavyweights only was taken by Ring Magazine in 1960. Amazingly enough, Rocky Marciano's name was not mentioned in their top ten. It wasn't until 1970 when Marciano's name appeared on most boxing writers' top ten lists. Obviously, the people of his generation gave him his rightful due when they were old enough to work as columnists.

Comparing one's ability and the impact a fighter had on society does not indicate how accomplished he is as a boxer. It is just as unfair to declare Mike Tyson greater than Evander Holyfield because he is considerably the more popular boxer of the two. Therefore, the fairest aspect to consider when rating a fighter's greatness would be what that fighter did during his career. What is relevant is who did they beat, how long they were considered top echelon, as well as any adversity that the fighter may have had to overcome (Foreman's physical age, Holyfield's size disadvantage) to achieve their success. Certainly having the ability to defeat a variety of fighters who possess conflicting styles and/or advantages proves how accomplished a fighter is as well. In this listing, I will explain what a fighter needed to accomplish in order to improve their status. When analyzing these elements, I'm sure you can agree to some extent to the fighters I have included in my personal top 10 list of greatest heavyweights.

1) Muhammad Ali

If you checked out each month's heavyweight ratings issued by Ring Magazine from 1963-1977, you could find at least 6 or 7 opponents within the top 10 that Ali defeated once or twice. Ali was 39 years old the first time he fought an opponent (Larry Holmes) he couldn't beat. Along the way, he won the heavyweight title on three occasions. Two of those victories were considered tremendous upsets over highly regarded physical specimens, Sonny Liston and George Foreman.

2) Joe Louis

Reigning for 11 ½ years with uninterrupted supremacy and 25 title defenses is certainly a credible criteria for being rated as high as he is. The only way he could have been "The Greatest" would have been not losing to Schmeling earlier in his career, or beating Charles or Marciano at the tail end of his career. Wins over Elmer Ray and a prime version of Jimmy Bivins may have improved his status as well.

3) Evander Holyfield

If you were to rank the best heavyweights from 1989-1999, you could find nearly everyone's name on Evander Holyfield's resume. After defeating Michael Dokes, one of the top 4 best heavyweights of the 80's, he then defended his number one status with two wins over #2 ranked fighters (never done or required by the top-ranked fighter). With the exception of Lennox Lewis, Holyfield defeated every fighter he faced as well as everyone who was perceived to be the best (Tyson, Bowe and Douglas) and won the heavyweight championship three times. Though he lost and drew with Lewis, the blemishes came at the tail end of his career against an opponent too big.

His other noted wins over Mercer, Foreman, Holmes and Moorer were considerable accomplishments. Holyfield was outweighed in all but one of his fights as a heavyweight and only Mike Tyson, Michael Moorer, Bobby Czyz and Seamus McDonaugh were heavyweights who scaled in under 220 pounds. Holyfield has also never faced an opponent who had a record under the .500 mark. No other heavyweight champion he succeeded had this distinction. Rocky Marciano went the distance with one of these opponents twice. If you also analyze his four losses, two of them were due to medical reasons: an obvious bum shoulder in his first fight with Moorer and suffering from hepatitis B in his third meeting with Bowe. What distinguishes him from fighters such as De la Hoya or Tyson is that he does not feel that cancellation is necessary when hampered by an injury. No matter what the circumstances are, he believes that he will have enough to win.

4) Larry Holmes

The dominance factor is there (21 title fight wins). The longevity is there, but he doesn't have enough quality opponents as the above fighters have despite his long career (from 1973-Present). Other than his impressive win over Ken Norton to win the title, he doesn't have that gargantuan victory. His win over Gerry Cooney was not as significant considering the fact that Cooney didn't fight competitively after the loss. Though he was 35 years old when he lost for the first time, it would come against blown-up, light-heavyweight champion, Michael Spinks.

5) George Foreman

Had Foreman not ducked Holmes for 20 years or defeated a worthy challenger (Tyson, Bowe, Lewis or Holyfield) of the 90's in his second reign as champion, he could have jumped to number two or three. Like Holmes, Foreman remained competitive into his 40's and became the oldest heavyweight champion when he knocked out Michael Moorer at the age of 45. Had Foreman faced a sturdier (chin-wise) champion however, he may not have accomplished that feat. The fighters I rated above Foreman also never lost to the caliber of an opponent like Jimmy Young who on any given day could lose to anyone.

6) Jack Johnson

Though he beat the best fighters of his day, he also lost to a few random opponents along the way in his physical prime. A one-eyed Marvin Hart for example was one of these fighters that reportedly licked Johnson.

Johnson's biggest wins against Sam Langford, Sam McVey and Joe Jeannette occurred when all of them were young and raw. McVey fought and lost to Johnson 3 times in 20 round fights, however, they happened within McVey's first 12 fights (also consider that these fighters did not have amateur experience). Johnson's win over Langford occurred when Langford was inexperienced as a heavyweight. Though Johnson showed competitiveness and fought into his 40's and even 50's, Holmes and Foreman were actually regarded as top ranked fighters at their advanced ages.

7) Rocky Marciano

Not only were most of his victories composed of washed up has-beens (even though they were the best available opponents), he reigned as champion for only four years and retired at the age of 32. The fighters I rated above him were either winning or defending their titles after that age. In spite of this, Marciano's first and last title fights spanned only 3 years of dominance (from his September '52 fight with Jersey Joe Walcott to his last fight with Archie Moore in September of '55). Therefore, the lack of longevity (which could have also added to his quality of opposition) is what hurts him most. As a result, you couldn't even complete a top ten list of his opponents without including fighters with an under .500 record. His record alone is what puts him into the top ten. You have to acknowledge and admire his consistency, though his record would have looked more glorified had he stayed around longer and defeated Floyd Patterson.

8) Joe Frazier

Though Frazier was dominant for four to five years during Ali's ring absence, he was pulverized (by George Foreman) before the age of 30. Holmes was once pulverized, however, it occurred when he was 38 and inactive for two years. Despite showing tremendous courage, Frazier did not fare too well when matched with a bigger, stronger opponent. Fighters such as Bonavena and Stander were also able to trouble or hurt Frazier because of their size. If Frazier couldn't go through you, he'd get stopped.

9) Mike Tyson

Tyson was thoroughly dominant from '86-90 and beat up every heavy-weight from the 80's with ease. If it weren't for Holmes' near title defense record, Tyson would have surpassed him as the best heavy-weight of the 80's. Despite being inactive through much of the 90's, he was always considered the best if not one of the best in the world when he was active. His biggest problem was coping with a boxer who wasn't afraid of him. Like Liston before him, Tyson's opponents were com-pletely terrified of him. Only three of his opponents thus far appeared as though they were not visibly afraid when fighting Tyson. The reason why this doesn't eliminate Tyson's status is because one of those fight-ers was one of the greatest (Holyfield) and the other (Buster Douglas) was a massive 6'4" heavyweight who possessed tremendous advantages.

10) Harry Wills

"The Black Panther" defeated one of the most accomplished fighters of all-time (Sam Langford) 16 of 18 times! He also beat every fighter will-ing to give him the chance (the more experienced versions of Sam McVey and Joe Jeannette). Despite being the number one contender from 1920-1926 he still never received his most deserved shot in spite of his ability and tremendous size. During that era his race (African-American) would have cancelled out his ability and prevented any title from being awarded to him.

Why Some Were Not Included!

Looking at my list, you would probably wonder why the infamous name of Jack Dempsey was not included. There are several reasons why he isn't. Consider that in his reign as champion (from 1919-1926), he was inactive for 4 of those years. He feasted on light-heavyweight com-petition (when heavyweights were available for him to fight) and was knocked cold once in the first round by Fireman Jim Flynn. Though being knocked out in one round doesn't eliminate a fighter from achieving greatness, no fighter listed above had ever experienced such an indignity. Though he came back the next year to reverse that verdict, his aura of invincibility was shattered. So he beat a behemoth in Jess Willard. Willard was inactive for nearly three years and could only fight haphazardly because of his size. Consider that during the two years before Dempsey became champion, he won one of five (1-2-2 record wise) contests against "Fat" Willie Meehan, a 210 pounder who should have been a middleweight. Middleweights such as Harry Greb had no problem beating the "Fatboy." Dempsey's detractors often criticized him for ducking Harry Wills.

What they should have done was crucify him. How can anyone make a top ten list without fighting the fighter deemed as the second best heavyweight (Wills) for seven years? If Dempsey is ranked at all, it's after Gene Tunney who whipped him twice.

Throughout the late 50's and early 60's, Sonny Liston wreaked havoc in the heavyweight division. While waiting for his earned shot at the title, Liston was beating the best available competition, some with relative ease. After he destroyed Floyd Patterson in his only two title fight victories, Liston's demise came quite abruptly. Though his downfall came against the great Muhammad Ali, he lost disgracefully in both fights against Ali's. Liston quit once and was stopped in the very first round the second time around. There are some that still believe that he quit in their return match as well.

Some would question the logic of having Evander Holyfield in the top 10 without including Riddick Bowe. Bowe twice defeated Holyfield in their three fight series, however he didn't beat many others. Like Marciano, you couldn't create a top ten list of quality opponents who Bowe defeated, and his reign (one-year) as well as his career (7 years) ended prematurely. Bowe had a tendency to fluctuate in weight in between fights and as a result, he wasn't sharp enough by fight time to utilize the wisdom and the guidance of Eddie Futch. His stoppage victory over Holyfield in their rubber match is also not too impressive considering the fact that he held tremendous size advantages in weight, height and reach. Holyfield was also ailing from the Hepatitis B virus.

A win over Mike Tyson or Lennox Lewis would have invited Bowe into the top 10.

Frank responds: Regarding Frazier, did we see the same fights? Bonavena was Frazier's 11th fight as pro and it was Bonavena's 30 something fights. Frazier is allowed to get stunned early by a crude strong veteran like Bonavena. As in regard to Stander, come on JD you're better than that. Frazier slipped. You saying if Frazier couldn't go through you he'd get stopped. Please tell me who could've whipped him like that other than maybe Liston. Your point about him being pulverized by Foreman before the age of 30 is senseless. Foreman would have beaten him at any age.

"*Foreman was 25 when Ali whipped him.
*Holyfield was not quite 30 when Bowe whipped him
*Louis was 21 when Schmeling whipped him
*Tyson was 23 when Douglas whipped him"

No these guys didn't get stopped in two rounds like Frazier did by Foreman. However if Holyfield, Louis, and Tyson faced the Foreman that Frazier did January 22, 1973 they would've met the same fate".

The best Frazier goes through Jack Johnson, Jack has nothing to keep Joe from walking through him. And Joe would pressure him too much to let Jack box him. Smoke stops skinny legs.

Frazier wears down Holmes and Holyfield, I love both Holmes and Holyfield.

But they couldn't handle pressure the way that Ali could. Frazier—Marciano—I can't see a smaller fighter than Frazier beating him. Frazier was also quicker than Marciano and Rocky was vulnerable to cuts. I know Frazier wasn't a cutting puncher but, as often as they would have hit each other it's not a reach to envision Rocky getting cut. At the worst if they fight 10 times Frazier gets a split ! At the Worst !

b) You are wrong about Foreman ducking Holmes in the 70s, you may be right in the 90s. I know for a fact that you're wrong about the 70s.

Foreman tried to fight Holmes after he came back from losing to Ali.

Foreman's people thought that Holmes (since his style was somewhat similar to Ali's) would be a good opponent to help Foreman prepare for a rematch with Ali. I know for a fact that Holmes' people turned it down. I forget the Italian guy's name who was managing Holmes at the time but, when that fight was offered in late 76 or early 77 he said "I'm not gonna ruin my fighter by putting him in with that animal". Richie Giachetti told me that back in 1977 at Deer Lake.

JD Responds: Guys, I think you skipped my criteria and went straight to my top 10. My ratings were based on career ACCOMPLISH-MENTS!

The whole basis of my rating greatness has little to do with comparing eras or how one guy from the 20's would do against a guy in the 60's. It's simply not fair. In my opinion, Frazier would go through Jack Johnson, Joe Louis, and Marciano. But he isn't as accomplished. If you read my criteria carefully you'll see that my rankings are not based on whom I believe could beat whom. Could Marciano beat Lennox Lewis? No! It's a physical mismatch. I'm a believer in evolution and therefore believe that fighters get better and better through the years. For example I believe Foreman was better in the 90's than he was in the 70's. Why? Because he was preserved, he got himself in better condition, hit just as hard if not harder and was more experienced.

When I said Foreman crushed Frazier before Frazier was 30, it meant that Frazier wasn't an old man when it happened and therefore, age would not be the reason why he was destroyed. When Holyfield loses to Ruiz, it has much to do with age, not the fact that Ruiz has the style to beat him. If Ruiz beat Holyfield when Holyfield was 28-32, I would think otherwise. I was trying to make the point that if you were a big puncher you had a great chance of beating Foreman. I believe Frazier would have lost to any big heavyweight who had a reasonably sturdy chin. Fortunately, for Frazier, he didn't face too many big guys during his career. Stander and Bonavena gave Frazier some trouble. And though Frazier fought Bonavena early on he was an Olympic champion, meaning being 11-0 meant that he was more of a 25-0 heavyweight for his time. The fact is he had to wail on Stander for a long time before the fight was stopped and Bonavena was able to hang in there with him. Neither Bonavena or Stander are big by today's standards but they were back then.

Frank counterattacks:

a.   I'm not sure I believe in evolution as much as you.

b.   Foreman of the 70s would have crushed Foreman of the 90s. Please say you don't believe Foreman of the 90s beats the 70s version. Not once in ten thousand tries. Patience would not have played a role. The young Foreman would have rolled over the old Foreman.

c.   Size is overrated. Holyfield and Tyson are proof. The two best since Holmes (1985) fought under 220 !

d.   You grossly underrate Frazier !

JD Vena: Primes are incomparable. God forbid, but let's say Shane Mosley died in a plane crash on the way to his first fight with Vernon Forrest. I bet that most would have falsely felt that Shane would have gone down as the best welterweight of his time. It's pure speculation, which is why comparing ones accomplishments are fair. Could Jack Johnson have beaten Jameel McCline? I doubt it very much. But how could you say McCline was greater. Accomplishments are the way to go. Of course they can be argued but it's easier and less speculative

Steve "Bucket" Gordan of Cyberboxingzone.com weighs in with his opinion of our list in an interview with Tom Donelson

Tom Donelson: How would you go about ranking Heavyweights?

Steve Gordan: I believe that we look at & judge fighters historically in their absolute primes. For Frazier that was March 8, 1971, in the first fight against Ali. On particular nights a fighter is invincible. The Joe Frazier of that night could have beaten most heavyweights in history. He was simply unstoppable.

For comparisons sake: The Louis that beat Schmelling in the rematch, The Dempsey that took Willard apart, The Holyfield that beat Tyson & Bowe in the 2nd fight, the Hagler that fought Hearns. On those particular nights these fighters were at their all time best and on those nights, I don't know who would have beaten them.

Tom Donelson: Your thoughts on Joe Frazier?

Steve Gordan: Back to Joe: That first fight with Ali ruined him. he was never the same again. I think he should be judged in his prime & in his prime, Joe Frazier was a man eating monster.

Tom Donelson: Give me some thoughts on Liston and Tyson.

Steve Gordan: The fact that Liston fell apart against a young Clay and could never put it together after that meant to me that he was a bum! When there was no plan B, as you like to call it, he gave up—Plain and simple. At least Tyson sucked it up in his first two losses but completely fell apart after his second defeat to Holyfield. Liston and Tyson should be called the humpty dumpty champions, but at least Tyson remained competitive during his post prime. Liston's level of dominance did not last very long. I'm just not big on guys who depend on intimidation as he and Tyson did.

Liston's rep was made during his reign of terror as a contender. For years Floyd Patterson wouldn't fight anybody and then he got in a long protracted series with Johannson. Liston treated the division as his own playground and was the best heavyweight in the world long before he won the title. By the time Liston dismantled Patterson he was already past his prime. So in retrospect what happened with him with Clay/Ali shouldn't have been a surprise. I rank Liston at #3 all-time after Ali & Holmes.

Tom Donelson: How about Foreman?

Steve Gordan: It took Foreman 13 years to recover from the Ali loss but he came back 100% stronger (mentally and physically) and in better condition. His confidence was there and he knew how to use his body unlike the way he fought in the 70's. The old Forman would throw punches to throw punches. If they landed, then they caused a devastating effect. In the 90's he knew how to set up punches.

Editor's note: After exhaustive debate, we finally agree upon a top 10 list for Heavyweights after 1930 and top five before 1930.

We both agreed that Ali was the greatest and Joe Louis was the second best heavyweight. After strong consideration, we moved Liston to number four and we tried to base this list on not just on a fighter's accomplishment but guessing whom would have been the better fighter in actual combat. For example, it was our opinion that Liston and Foreman were too strong for Marciano or Frazier. We are still unsure about Holmes' place in history, but we feel that his ability as a fighter has been unappreciated. Fighting in the shadow of Ali, Holmes never was given his due. We need more time to sort out Lewis' and Holyfield's place in boxing history. There is no doubt that both Holyfield and Lewis belong in the top 10 heavyweights since the 1930's. Tyson, on the other hand, is more difficult to rank. He had the talent to match up with Rocky Marciano and Joe Frazier, but did he have the intangibles? We included responses from Bill Chair, JD Vena and Steve Gordan of Cyberboxing.com to add some extra perspective and differing opinions. As one can see, it is a difficult process to select the greatest. Opinions differ.

Interview with Tracy Callis

By Tom Donelson

Tracy Callis is one of the leading experts on the older boxers, pre 1930's era. He has written extensively on these fighters and believes that these fighters were better than given credit. This interview was part of a series of exchanges dealing with how modern day boxers would compare to the older fighters at the turn of the last century. Mr. Callis has no doubt that the older fighters such as Dempsey, Jack Johnson and Jim Jefferies would compare favorably to the great fighters of the past half-century including Joe Louis and Muhammad Ali.

Tom Donelson: Give me some background on your interest in boxing.

Tracy Callis: I have been researching boxing history and the records of boxers for 40 years and work on producing rare updated records for many older boxers. I have a strong interest in boxers of all weight classes from every historical period.

I am presently the Director of Historical Research for The Cyberboxingzone (Cyberboxingzone.com) and an Elector for the International Boxing Hall of Fame. I am also a member of the International Boxing Research Organization (IBRO), a contributor to the British Boxing Board of Control Record Book, a member of the newly formed Historical Society of Black Prizefighters (HSBP), and a member of the Roanoke (Virginia) Boxing Club where I presently live.

In my capacity for The Cyberboxingzone, I am the leading researcher and historian. The site has 350,000 viewers per month.

Tom Donelson: How do you go about deciding the best and how do the rules of early years of boxing affect ratings?

Tracy Callis: You are absolutely correct about rules and their effect upon the way bouts are fought. Do you consider them when evaluating the fighters against each other? Who would win under the old conditions (grabbing, holding, hitting, infighting) as well as the modern rules? I have a massive collection of the following:

Boxing Films (old and modern)—I have watched these hundreds of times. In addition I have studied questionnaires from fellow boxing experts and writers. I have studied and assessed these many, many times.

With my computer and mathematical background, I have written several computer simulators to match profiles for the various men. Some interesting characteristics surfaced. I use the following statistical comparisons—Win Percentage, KO Percentage, Relative Win Percentage, Relative KO Percentage, Projected Win Percentage, Win Percentage By Weight, KO Percentage By Weight, Win Percentage By Height, KO Percentage By Height, Win Percentage By Girth, KO Percentage By Girth, Win Percentage By Era, KO Percentage By Era.

"Size, weight, strength, and power" are important in boxing. Those with it are to be avoided whereas those without it need to cultivate skills to avoid the men with it. Boxing skills offset "size, weight, strength, and power" but when the skills are not perfected or sufficient, then "size, weight, strength, and power" again becomes a strong factor in who will win a fight. Men like Dempsey, Tunney, Fitzsimmons, and Corbett did not need to be 230 lbs. (as you mention) to be dominant. Lighter men are usually quicker. Heavier men are usually slower but probably stronger. Of course, there are no absolutes here, only probabilities.

Dempsey and Louis had the capability to handle larger, heavier, bigger men (in the clinches too). Smaller, lighter fighter, who could match Ali's quickness, proved difficult for Ali. Further, I would argue that the primary boxing tactics were in place by the late teens with only minor improvements.

Finally, I make the statement that athletes, like people, are bigger, stronger, faster but (after following sports for 53 years) it is apparent to me they play the game "dumber." Perfected techniques can overcome nature and improve man's performance. But, in man against man sports, it is action-reaction that determines winners and this does not always translate into bigger, faster, stronger.

Tom Donelson: What qualities do the greatest have?
Tracy Callis: The qualities needed to be a great fighter are speed, quickness, stamina, strength, hitting power, chin (ability to take punishment), native boxing "savvy" (action-reaction type of thing), good hands, determination, heart, hunger. I believe Jefferies and most of the old timers had these characteristics. I do not believe the moderns have these—only some of them and in varying degrees). The "ACID TEST" is the ability to take that KO punch when it hits a man!

Old timers were in condition both mentally and physically whereas today's men are not (generally speaking). We see some very "competitive" fights today but that is because today's fighters are nearly equal and competitive. This does not translate into greatness. In my judgment, Corbett was the fastest man to ever fight as heavyweight, not Ali. Corbett fought at his pace for 15-20 rounds whereas Ali slowed considerably after 6-7 rounds. Jim Jefferies when he fought Tom Sharkey for the title, fought with an injured arm and the Medical doctors wanted to put the bout off. Jefferies said no and beat Sharkey, a Marciano's clone, with his best weapon unavailable.

Tom Donelson: What do older fighters have in your opinion that modern day fighters do not have?
Tracy Callis: I repeat, the qualities needed to be a great fighter are speed, quickness, stamina, strength, hitting power, chin (ability to take punishment), native boxing "savvy" (action-reaction type of thing),

good hands, determination, heart, hunger. I believe Jeffries and most of the old timers had these characteristics. I do not believe the moderns have these—especially hunger, heart, and conditioning.

There is an article from the Journal of Sociology that I referenced in one of my Cyberboxingzone articles. It speaks of socio-economic conditions and how it affects boxers. As we go back further into American history, we find people of all races enduring hardships and, in general, "living without" and toughing it out. This goes for whites as well as blacks. So, old-time whites went through what the blacks go through as far as socio conditioning. The "scratch-and-claw" socio-economic conditions produce better fighters. This is one reason whites are not as prevalent as they once were.

Tom Donelson: Many of the older fighters had many no-decisions on their records due to state regulations that did not count fights not ending in a knockout. How do you judge the older fighters, if the early records are not as accurate as they should be?

Tracy Callis: I have a large collection of old timer films, newspaper clippings, and microfilm to study. Whereas the older fighters were not as polished as many moderns, they exhibited wonderful spunk and stamina. Moderns, with all their latest technique, tend to be in less than best condition and slow considerably over the course of a fight

Tom Donelson: What was special about Jack Johnson and Bob Fitzsimmons, who you pick as the best pound for pound?

Tracy Callis: Johnson was a wonderful defensive fighter who carried his man more often than not (to be in the spotlight). He possessed a quick, sharp mean jab and uppercut. He fought "flat-footed" but could move with extreme quickness when necessary. I believe he could have KO'd 80 percent of his foes had he wanted.

Not only did Fitz defeat Corbett, he defeated Nonpareil Jack Dempsey, hammered Jim Jeffries twice, and KO'd many heavyweights while he weighed around 165-175 pounds. Most Light heavies faded against heavies, but not Fitz.

Tom Donelson: What did you like about Jack Dempsey?

Tracy Callis: I do not believe Jack Dempsey to be overrated. He was fast (ran 100 yards in less than ten seconds), powerful, aggressive (much more so than Joe Louis), hit hard in combinations and with both hands, was rugged and had a good chin. He was an excellent boxer, who could bob and weave. He fought from a crouch (troublesome for most fighters). Also, in my view, his opposition was better than that of Joe Louis, Rocky Marciano, and a number of other champions.

As Henry Cooper once said, the ability to hit extremely hard is a God-given talent and does not have much to do with lifting weights. Weights make you strong but are not the primary factor in making a fighter a true knockout hitter. Dempsey, Louis, Fitzsimmons, Marciano, Sullivan, Tom Sharkey, Mike Tyson, and Joe Frazier had this talent among the lighter heavyweights. Of course, Jim Jeffries, Jess Willard, Max Baer, Sonny Liston, and George Foreman had that God-given ability among the larger men.

Dempsey and Tunney had excellent skills and techniques, probably better than most of their predecessors. However, other fighters had some natural skills (in abundance) which more than compensated for lack of skill in some areas—Corbett with his exceptional "jack-rabbit" quickness, Fitzsimmons with his craftiness and abnormal hitting talent, Jeffries with his strength, power, stamina, and chin, Johnson with his quick, wicked jab and uppercut and quickness of foot from a flat-footed position.

Tom Donelson: I agree with you that Gene Tunney was an excellent boxer. Why do you think others refuse to give enough credit to Tunney?

Tracy Callis: Tunney was an excellent technician who was smart, well disciplined, fast, and carried a stiff punch. However, he was "not color-ful" and this hurt his image. He read a lot (Shakespeare, etc.) and this was not the concept of a rugged pugilist in the mind of the public. And, finally, he beat Dempsey, a colorful champion who was very pop-ular, and this detracted from his popularity also.

As good as Gene was, Jack was better. Jack boxed well, fought from the crouch (and moved very quickly in doing so), hit with dynamite in both hands-rugged, and aggressive (which forced opponents to react fast and likely to somewhere make a mistake that would enable him to get in his hard "punches in bunches").

Tom Donelson: You rank Sugar Ray Robinson the top welterweight but only number five as middleweight, what was your rationale in put-ting him at number five as a Middle Weight?
Tracy Callis: Robinson was an all-time great as a welterweight and middleweight. He just wasn't as good as middleweight as welterweight. Check his record as a welterweight and middleweight. Yes, he was older when he fought as a middleweight and he was very good. In abso-lute pure talent though, there were better men in the middleweight division.

I rate Bob Fitzsimmons above Ray as a "pound-for-pound" fighter. He fought anyone, regardless of weight, all through his career. He won the middleweight, heavyweight, and light-heavyweight titles. He was crafty and coy (like old Archie Moore) and recuperated well from blows. In my judgment, he was an exceptional hitter and hit much harder than Ray.

Tom Donelson: You were impressed with Jefferies. Do you think that Jefferies could have beaten Jack Johnson if both fought at their peak?
Tracy Callis: In my opinion, Jeffries would defeat Johnson if they both fought at their peaks. Too much strength, power, stamina along with his crouch and chin. All battles would be close though. Jeffries

was an all-around athlete, not the slow and ponderous plodder that he is portrayed as today.

Jefferies was ranked #1 All-Time by many polls (correction: most polls) up to the 1950's when Nat Fleischer came out with his ratings. Johnson was #1 and Jeffries #2. Nat had seen the fight between the two men and obviously was impressed by Johnson. That fight was hardly fair to Jeffries who had not fought in six years, came down from 300 pounds to around 230. Johnson had 42 bouts since Jeff retired and was at his peak. The temperature was about 110 degrees that day. So, Jeff was sluggish and second best—hardly in shape to be impressive.

Tom Donelson: What qualities did Jefferies possess that would make him your number one Heavyweight champion? How do you view Ali?
Tracy Callis: Ali was a very, very good boxer. The best since Joe Louis. But, in my opinion, he is overrated and to lose to someone like Leon Spinks under any condition, my goodness. Jefferies, Johnson, Louis, Dempsey would never have lost to Spinks, even on their worst day in the ring.

My problem with Ali as the greatest is (1) he did little infighting, (2) he did little or no body punching, (3) he had trouble with men who crouched, (4) he was fortunate because he fought men who rarely crouched (a troublesome style), (5) he fought big punchers who followed him around the ring pretty much in a straight up position (ideal for a fast jabbing sharpshooter like Ali), (6) most of his foes followed him in a straight line, failing to cut the ring off, (7) the big men he fought tended to lack stamina and run out of gas about round 6-7 or so, (8) he had considerable trouble with smaller, quicker men like Doug Jones, Henry Cooper, Leon Spinks, Jimmy Young (most of the great fighters of the past were smaller and quicker), (9) his record was 56-5 and, in my judgment, could/should have been 52-9 (probable losses to Cooper except for a split glove and time delay; Kenny Norton—all three bouts; Joe Frazier—first two bouts; Jimmy Young)

Jefferies was (1) approximately the same size as Liston and Foreman, (2) was as strong and powerful as they, (3) hit like they did, (4) had as tough or tougher chin than either, (5) had far greater stamina AND faster footwork than either, (6) fought from a crouch, (7) was patient—didn't punch himself out, (8) was used to fighting "boxer types" since Corbett and Fitzsimmons were of that type (and he fought them in a larger ring than 16x16 so he was familiar with tracking down lighter, faster, quicker men)

Tom Donelson: How do styles effect fights?
Tracy Callis: Styles make fights and offer a distinct advantage/disadvantage to particular fighters depending upon the match-up. The basic styles are boxer, slugger, swarmer, and boxer-puncher.

Boxer type generally beats the Slugger (too quick for the heavy hitter big man; Corbett, Tunney, Johnson, Ali)

Slugger generally beats the Swarmer (too big and strong for the strong but smaller man; Liston, Foreman; Jefferies—but more than a slugger).

Swarmer generally beats the Boxer type (strong but small enough with stamina to hang on until the boxer slows down; Frazier, Marciano, Tyson, Tom Sharkey, John L. Sullivan)

Boxer-Puncher (a variety of skills; he matches up well against all other types because he can change; most of your all-time best are of this style; Dempsey, Louis, Holmes, perhaps Johnson and Ali)

It is likely (probable) that the very best of any era could fight with the very best of any other era. It is likely (probable) that no single fighter could beat all the others or beat all the others every time (among the very best).

Anatomy of the Knockout

By Tom Donelson
Published in Cyberboxingzone.com May, 2002

A kickboxer once told me about the first time he was knocked out. "I was getting ready to unleash a right-hand, when I got nailed by a left hook'"he told me, "all I could remember afterwards was my seconds helping me up and seeing my opponent celebrating." There is nothing more dramatic in sports than the knockout. With a quick flick of the wrist, the glove makes contact with the opponent's face and all the brain's synapses misfire. The recipient of the knockout never sees the shot that sends him to the canvas and is rarely aware of the surroundings around him. There is no pain, just embarrassment. The pain comes later.

Floyd Patterson's strategy against Ingemar Johansson in their first fight was to use his quickness against the taller Swede. Floyd's own thoughts before his knockout was, "This guy is nothing. I'm going to go in and just throw combinations and gamble. He may catch me with one or two, but I'll catch him with five or six and that will be it. I'll knock him out." Patterson went to throw his combinations and before he knew it, he was down. Patterson did not even remember the knockout. As Patterson recalled, "I just remember the referee saying, "Neutral corner," I said, I must have knocked him down, so I went to go to a neutral corner. That is when Ingemar came up and caught me again and I realized that it was me who was going down."

Patterson did not remember much of that fateful round as he lost his championship for the first time. As Patterson noted, "you do not feel the pain. To me, it was a lovable feeling. Maybe its like dope, I don't know…It's like you're floating." The fighter's receptor sites are no longer functioning and he is never quite sure of where he is. Instinct takes over but sometimes that is not enough.

Joe Louis recalls that after being knocked down in the second round against Schmeling, "I really didn't know what happened the rest of the fight. I didn't know nothing, I didn't know where I was, nothing…The only thing I remember when I went out of the ring, my trainer, Manny Seamon, saying, cover his face because my face, my jaw was out like this, where I had stopped so many right hands that night." Louis fought another 10 rounds against the right-handed-minded German and never remembered the rest of the fight. It was animal instinct that kept him in the fight for a boxer trains by repetition and this repetition takes over when the memory ceases to work. Louis fought most of the fight, by memory. That is one effect of the knockdown.

Jack Sharkey came up with memories of a dead colleague when Primero Carnera knocked him out. When he hit the canvas, "I looked and I saw vision of Ernie Schaaf (who previously was killed in the ring after being KO'd by Carnera). There was no pain, just a feeling of turmoil momentum, a constant buzz saw going around." Sharkey remembers his last fight with the great Joe Louis. Louis began the fight like a buzz saw and dominated the early part of the fight. Sharkey's strategy was to play counterpuncher, waiting to catch Louis at the right moment. Sharkey was waiting for the right time when Louis right hand ended the proceeding. Sharkey recalls after the knockout, "I'm looking off at the audience I snapped out of it, witnessed the proceedings as they raised Louis hands." Sharkey merely threw kisses as he left the ring, not having seen the punch that ended his career. All he could remember was Joe Louis with his hands raised in victory.

Former light heavyweight Tommy Loughran told an interviewer that," I don't care who you are and how great you are, you're going to get hit." A boxer's lot in life is to get hit and even the great ones hit the canvas. Ali, Marciano, and Louis—they all felt the taste of leather and all were knocked down.

Sometimes there are the brutal knockouts in which the end is inevitable and the only thing keeping up the losing fighter is guts and courage. James J. Braddock defended his championship against Joe Louis and for eight rounds, he felt the blow of every sledgehammer shot of Joe Louis. Going into the eighth round, Braddock was taking a savage beating and his face needed 23 stitches after the fight. Braddock remembers being hit by a right hand that drove "the tooth through the mouthpiece and right through the lip." Braddock concluded that Louis' power was such, "when he knocked me down, I could have stayed there for three weeks." For Braddock, who admitted that Joe Louis hit him more times than any other fighter, the knockout was a merciful end. It was like being guillotined after being tortured, the final ending coming with no pain after enduring punch after punch.

A fighter feels more humiliated than hurt after being knocked out. Patterson sunk into depression after his knockout loss to Johansson but he later returned the favor when he knocked out the big Swede. Seeing films of that knockout still sends shivers down my spine. Johansson was nailed with a left hook and when it was over, the only things moving were his feet, twitching. Patterson, for one brief moment, thought he killed his opponent. As for Johansson, there was no memory of the end. No pain and no memory, a typical knockout.

The knockout is a dramatic moment that climaxes a boxing match. It is the exclamation point of the boxing match that sends excitement throughout the stands. As for the victim of the knockout, there is no memory of the event, only disbelief as the fight is replayed on the morning news the next day.

When Validation lacks Validity

By Frank J. Lotierzo

(Editor notes: This was written before the Tyson-Lewis and its place in history. This was Published in the May issue of Wail.)

Hey, are you going to the big fight ? What big fight ! Can't be Ali-Frazier 1, because that was the biggest fight. No not that one. Oh you mean Leonard-Hearns, no not that one. Oh you must mean Pryor-Arguello, no not that one either. I'll give you a hint: by today's standards it's a big fight and it's not Hopkins-Trinidad. Still don't know? Maybe this will help. Fighter X was knocked out eight years ago by one punch delivered courtesy of a tough journeyman, and knocked out by one punch last year by a glorified journeyman. Fighter Y was knocked out twelve years ago by an in-shape journeyman, then followed that up six years later by getting knocked out by a former great who had to get clearance from the Mayo Clinic. The following year, he fought the same former great champion but didn't get knocked out that time. He quit before he was knocked out. Oh I know what fight you are talking about, it must be Lewis-Tyson. Yes that is the fight. Is that really a big fight? Yes, by today's standards it's world war three! Those are the credentials that fighters can have today which constitutes a major PPV fight.

Most of the hard core fight fans and top boxing scribes are really pumped up for Lewis-Tyson. Yes, it is Lewis-Tyson, not Tyson-Lewis because Lewis is still Heavyweight Champion. There is talk by those just mentioned that the winner of this bout will have validated himself as one of the all-time great heavyweight champions. What a myth that is. Regardless of who wins or how decisive, I wish this fight would

101

never come off. It tires me just anticipating how many times I will have to explain this very simple equation. If you think that either Lewis or Tyson should have their mug atop boxing's version of Mount Rushmore, you better put that drink down and tip the bartender before asking him to call a cab to take you home! Here's the problem. If you don't think that Lewis' or Tyson's mug is already on boxing's highest mountain top before their hands are wrapped, gloves tied, and have made the traditional ring entrance, then a win in this fight should not be the launching pad.

Of course, a Lewis-Tyson Fight is not guaranteed. It's 64 days away as of this writing. Let's just say the fight happens and Lewis demolishes Tyson the way Hearns did Cuaves. Big deal! So he KO'd a fighter who was not only the youngest to become Heavyweight Champion, but also the youngest to become a former Heavyweight Champion. Yes, that would be the Buster Douglas fight, twelve years ago. Don't tell me Tyson lost because he was out of shape. If I said to you before the fight that Douglas is in the best shape of his life and Tyson is in the worst shape of his career, would you have picked Douglas to knock out Tyson? No way would you pick the 42 to 1 underdog Douglas. If Tyson was so out of shape, how did he drop Douglas in the eighth round after taking a beating for the first seven and three quarter rounds? No excuse here, he got battered. Six years later he was beaten by former Heavyweight Champ Evander Holyfield who was coming off the two worst fights of his career, (being KO'd by Bowe in their third fight and having life and death trying to floor former middle-weight Bobby Czyz).

We all know that Tyson only agreed to fight Holyfield because he appeared to be a dead man walking. I don't want to hear that Tyson was more spent than Holyfield, lest we forget Holyfield is four years older and has taken much more punishment throughout his career. Tyson will have everything that he's wanted, a win over Holyfield to put on his record. Even a shot Holyfield will do. Tyson was no dummy. He knew that no one will say it was a shot Holyfield, they'll just know Tyson beat Holyfield. He couldn't be more wrong if he tried. Not only does Holyfield put him down in round six, he kicks his ass for ten rounds before stopping him in round eleven. Seven months later after one postponement they meet again. Once again, Tyson can't fall back on the excuse that he took Holyfield lightly. For two rounds, as in the first fight, Holyfield is getting the better of it. Tyson feels it is only a matter of rounds before Holyfield stopped him a second time. As I said Tyson was no dummy. In the middle of the third round Tyson cried to referee Mills Lane that Holyfield was butting him. How bout that, the dirtiest fighting Heavyweight Champion of all time was pleading with the ref about the bully Evander Holyfield.

When Lane didn't fall for it, Tyson now was desperate to find a way out. What did the baddest man on the planet do? He bit Holyfield's ear. After a firm warning from Lane who told him he will DQ him if he did it again, what does Iron Mike do the next time they clinch? He bit again! Fight Over! Holyfield wins! Tyson fought in 1996 and 1997. Since Holyfield ll, Tyson hasn't fought anyone worth the paper on which this is written. So, you tell me why Lennox Lewis would secure his mug on boxing's Mount Rushmore by beating Tyson. He only beat a fighter who was Ko'd twelve years ago by a journeyman, and was stopped by a fading former champ six years later. Oh yes, they did fight again, and as I said, Tyson is no dummy. He quit before he was stopped. So you try and tell me how Lewis validates himself with a victory over Tyson. It's not like it's never happened before. This isn't Ali over Liston, or Frazier over Ali, and it is certainly not Foreman over Frazier. It's just Lewis over Tyson. Been there done that. Some validation !

What if the fight goes the other way? What if Tyson beats Lewis as Hagler beat Hearns. Big deal! So he stops a fighter who will probably be remembered for possessing the softest chin since Floyd Patterson. Floyd at least had a real excuse—he was a small heavyweight. Lewis can't say that, not when you're 6'5" and over 240 lbs. How many former Heavyweight Champions can you think of who lost their title by one punch, not once but twice! Not an easy task to even come up with another. And it's not like he was hit by Joe Louis of 1937 or George Foreman of 1973. It was Oliver McCall, a tough journeyman. Try and come up with a name heavyweight he beat that would be considered a third tier heavyweight other than Lewis. This is the same Oliver McCall who less than a year later won a disputed decision, I mean a really disputed decision, over Larry Holmes. Would be a heck of a feat, if Holmes wasn't 45 years old. Think about that one! McCall knocks out Lennox Lewis in two rounds and in his next fight is taken twelve rounds to a disputed decision victory over an old Holmes. What this says is that the 28 year old Lewis is counted out in two rounds by the same fighter who in his next fight can only win a disputed decision over the 45 year old Holmes. What would Holmes in his prime have done to Lewis, It's a scary thought. Just in case you forgot, McCall's one punch knockout of Lewis was just eight years ago. I must mention that Lewis did exact some revenge over McCall. Remember that fight, when McCall walked in to the ring crying because he was in the ring instead of a drug rehab? Tell me the monumental feat Tyson will achieve with a knockout over Lewis, and we're not done yet. Correct me if I'm wrong, but wasn't Lewis KO'd by some guy named Hasim Rahman last year?

Oh I almost forgot, as hard as this is to believe it was also by one punch. As I said Tyson is no dummy. When Lewis goes, he really goes. The ref better have ten fingers and maybe at least five toes when he's called for a Lewis fight. Wasn't this Rahman guy knocked out and out of the ring by the Russian bear Oleg Maskaev? Yeah, he's the one. It must be said however that Lewis did repay Rahman by knocking him out in the rematch. Lewis, unlike Tyson, gets the W the second time around with his conqueror. However, we can't dismiss Lewis being KO'd for the ten count last year. So what does a knockout of Lewis by Tyson prove? It's not like it hasn't been done before. It was done eight years ago, and also just last year. What Tyson will prove is that he could knockout a fighter that was KO'd by McCall eight years ago, and a fighter who was knocked out last year by Rahman. Once again, it's not like Tyson would be stopping an Ali or a Foreman or Frazier. Come on, George Chuvalo and Tex Cobb on their worst day go the entire distance with McCall and Rahman. But Lewis didn't!

Here's the problem with trying to build a case for the Mount Rushmore of boxing. What is the earth shattering accomplishment? Lewis was KO'd eight years ago by McCall, and just last year by Rahman. A Tyson's victory would be no big deal. Same with Lewis, a victory would confirm that he knocked out the same guy that Buster Douglas did twelve years ago, and a washed up Holyfield did six years ago. If people thought Holyfield beat a shell of a Tyson, which he didn't, what's the news if Lewis beats Tyson six years after Holyfield? All this will tell us is that Lennox Lewis beat Mike Tyson. It's been done. If you think that the victor in the Lewis—Tyson fight validates an all time top ten ranking, you haven't been following the fight game long enough, or you just don't know what you are watching. Or you can say you stayed at the bar too long and you were debating Jack Daniels. Some validation, Mr Lewis and Mr.Tyson. If you're starved for validation, go to your fight films and play anyone of the following tapes !

Frazier defeating the undefeated Ali in Super Fight 1, Foreman defeating the undefeated Frazier in Jamaica, Ali defeating the undefeated Foreman "In the Rumble in the jungle", Duran defeating the undefeated Leonard "in the Brawl for it all", Leonard defeating the undefeated Hearns "In The Showdown", Hopkins defeating the undefeated Trinidad.

These are signature fights which validate true greatness. Lewis—Tyson should never make this list!!

Ward And Gatti: A Throwback To Old Days

By Tom Donelson

Editor's note: Micky Ward and Arthur Gatti fought a brutal ten round fight on May 18th, 2002. The fight was close with Ward eking out a close decision that could have gone either way. This fight had an ebb and flow with each fighter taking command at specific points of the fight, with each fighter giving and taking from one another. Neither fighter at this point in their career will be champion but they are still capable of making big money since they have a loyal following who appreciate their courage and non-stop action style.

It was a fight that could have easily been taped in black and white, a throwback to the old days. "Irish" Micky Ward and Arturo "Thunder" Gatti simply brawled for 10 rounds. Gatti, using his quickness and superior boxing skills, attempted to box his way to victory but Ward soon turn this boxing match into a street brawl. Gatti won the first three rounds by maneuvering around the slower Ward but by the fourth round, Ward imposed his will upon Gatti. Gatti reverted back to his own brawling past and deserted his boxing strategy. From the fourth round on, Gatti and Ward exchanged punch after punch. Punches were flying at a record pace as both men eschewed defense.

The ninth round proved to be the decisive round of the fight. Ward was wearing Gatti down in the previous rounds with body shots and needed a big round to score a victory. Ward let loose with a ferocious assault of head and body punches. Gatti hit the floor after receiving a vicious left hook to the body. Gatti, like Ward, is a warrior and he would not stay down. Ward continued his assault, as Gatti appeared to be out on his feet. Somehow Gatti survived the round barely on his feet as the bell ended the round. Buddy McGirt, Gatti's trainer, nearly stopped the fight as his boxer could barely get up to start the tenth round. The fight could easily have been stopped and in most cases, would have been. Only Gatti's reputation allowed the fight to continue.

Gatti's courage allowed him to start the 10th round. The two warriors, exhausted by their battle, slowly came out to begin the 10th round. After touching gloves, they went to work on each other. Ward could not finish the job that he started in the 9th and Gatti showed why he is nicknamed "Thunder." Gatti not only survived the tenth but won the round. It was not enough though to secure the decision.

Over the years, Gatti has been in many wars and his face shows the result. At the age of 30, Gatti's best years are long past him—the victim of too many wars. The real question is how many wars can a fighter survive before the body runs out? For Gatti, his championship days are long since past and he is now slowly slipping into journeyman territory. There are just so many punches that a body can survive before the body rebels.

At the age of 36, Micky Ward is now in a position to command more lucrative paychecks and certainly, Mr. Ward deserves bigger paydays based on his past performances. Both of these fighters are action fighters. They give everything they have and leave nothing on the ring floor. That is why both fighters are routinely featured on television revues. They never fail to give a rousing performance and this fight was no exception.

There is a scene in the first "Rocky" film, in which Rocky's character is reviewing the ring the night before the big fight. The promoter advances to Rocky and tells Rocky that he will provide a good show. At this point, Rocky fully understands that he is merely a foil in Apollo Creed's fight. It is Rocky's job to provide a competitive fight and take his lumps. That is Gatti and Ward to a T. These fighters are entertainers, who provide the fans their pound of flesh.

This fight was as close as any fight could be as Ward streaked out a close decision but this fight could have gone the other way. Fights like this however have a cost. Wars like the Gatti-Ward shortens careers. When Ali fought Frazier, these fights changed both men and took years from their careers. The third Ali-Frazier was both fighters' last great moment as their skills quickly eroded after their fight in Manila. While Ali would continue to be a champion for three more years, his erosion of skills became evident with each passing fight. Ali's loss to Leon Spinks in their fight was as much the result of his war against Frazier. Frazier would have two more fight, a knockout loss to George Foreman and the other a draw before retiring.

The war between Gatti and Ward will eventually show its scars in later fights. Gatti's face is made up of scar tissues as his past wars have slowed his reflexes and the quickness that characterized his early career is disappearing. At the age of 30, Gatti is an old fighter. He has been involved in too many wars and physically he is closer to 40 than his real age. Ward has but a few good fights left and at the age of 36, he has little time to take advantage of his new box office appeal. Ward's fate is similar to Gatti's, he is trapped by his tough man reputation. He will fight the latest and toughest guy but age and his share of boxing's war will soon sap his strength and skill as a fighter. He will never be a champion but boxing fans could care less. For the Gattis and Wards of the world provide modern day boxing fans their glimpse of past history. In the 50's, boxing was regular staple on television and wars like Gatti—Ward were a common everyday occurance.

Gatti and Ward are the last of a breed, bangers who show no concern for their bodies. For these fighters understand their role, hit and be hit. As both fighters slide on the downside of their career, their courage allows them to collect big paycheck. Gatti and Ward have paid physical price for the entertainment of boxing fans. Both fighters have long since sacrificed their bodies to pursue a dream—a shot at a title.

Gatti already has his belt but he still wants one more chance at championship glory. But too many wars have diminished both fighters skills and all they have left is heart and courage. Both fighters sacrifice all for their craft and the fans appreciate these warriors. They are the last warriors, ready for war and ready to throw and catch punches.

Michael Spinks: A Real Champion

By Frank Lotierzo

When Michael Spinks won his Olympic gold medal at the 1976 Olympics in Montreal, he was overshadowed by his older brother Leon, who also won a gold medal. When Leon owned the undisputed World Heavyweight title from a severely eroded Muhammad Ali, once again Michael was overshadowed. Yet at the conclusion of his career, Michael Spinks would be the first light heavyweight to challenge and defeat the sitting heavyweight champion. His brother would retire a forgotten journeyman fighter with barely a .500 record.

Spinks' brilliant career came close to never being realized. Coming out of the 1976 Olympics, boxing was a third priority for Michael Spinks. First was maintaining his job at a chemical plant to help take care of his mother in St. Louis. There was no big contract offer waiting for a signature to turn professional. Second was that Leon came out of the Olympics with more promise and expectation. Those who followed the brothers' amateur careers more closely felt that Michael had the more promising career, and had a style more suited to the pro game. However, Leon was streaking his way to becoming a ranked heavyweight contender, and becoming a television staple of ABC sports.

ABC capitalized on having broadcast the summer Olympics by showcasing the five American boxers who captured gold. Michael's career was pushed to the back burner. Convinced by flamboyant boxing promoter Butch Lewis in 1977, Spinks turned pro. On April 17, 1977, Michael Spinks won his first fight. This would be the launching pad for one of the most productive and successful boxing careers in the history of the Light Heavyweight division. Spinks brought to the division a style that could be a real pain if you were fighting in the Light Heavyweight division. He was almost 6″3″ with a seventy nine-inch reach, only two inches shorter than Larry Holmes. He had a good long hard jab and his left hook, as well as his left uppercut were devastating punches. Let's not forget the "Spinks jinx" in the right hand. He scored some devastating knockouts with the Spinks jinx—Marvin Johnson, Yaqui Lopez, Jerry Celestine were some of his notable victims. Spinks could also box from the outside, as Eddie Mustafa Muhammad and Dwight Muhammad Qawi would attest. In his unification bout with the iron man Qawi, Spinks' back touched the rope only once in 15 rounds.

Spinks blazed through his first sixteen fights which included knockout victories over former two-time Light Heavyweight Marvin Johnson and veteran contender Yaqui Lopez. Spinks then challenged Eddie Mustafa Muhammad for the WBA's light heavyweight crown. Mustafa would be Spinks biggest challenge. Muhammad came into this bout in tremendous condition and started off fast, taking advantage of vast experience and his cunning boxing skills. Spinks fell behind early in the fight and was shut out going into round five. From the fifth round, Spinks controlled the fight by forcing the champion to follow him and setting up the champion to be hit with all of Spinks' arsenal. He used uppercuts and overhand rights to the pressuring Muhammad. Going into the twelfth round, the champion was cut and bleeding and fell victim to the Spinks' jinx. A Spinks' right hand sent the champion sprawling to the canvas. Muhammad rose to finish the fight but lost a unanimous decision to the new champion Michael Spinks. Spinks defended his WBA championship by scoring five straight kayos. Spinks beat the division best including top ranked contender Vonzell Johnson and the tough Murray Sutherland.

Spinks' next challenge was Dwight Qawi, who won his version of the title by knocking out Matthew Saad Muhammad. Qawi scored three knockouts in a row, including a rematch victory over Matthew

Saad Muhammad. On March 18th, Michael Spinks and Dwight Muhammad Qawi meet for the undisputed Light Heavyweight championship of the world. Both fighters creamed the entire division, scoring impressive wins over the best of the best. Spinks was undefeated and the once beaten Qawi hadn't lost since dropping a six round decision to Johnny Davis in his third bout as a pro. This fight presented two fighters with contrasting styles. Qawi did his best work on the inside, ripping the body with bone jarring hooks and right uppercuts to the chin, but he was an underrated boxer. Spinks looked to box, using his height advantage but Spinks could really punch. The fight was close but Spinks prevailed in a 15 round majority decision to claim the undisputed Light Heavyweight championship of the world. Spinks demonstrated his versatility against his best opponent to date. In this fight, Michael Spinks put on a clinic on how to use the jab; to keep the hard charging Qawi from coming at him with impunity. Spinks proceeded to clean out the division over the next two years. Having run out of worthy challengers in his true division, and having one of the most complete careers in Light Heavyweight history, Spinks heard the call of the Heavyweight dollars.

Looking to build upon his legacy, Spinks relinquished his Light Heavyweight title to challenge the current undefeated Heavyweight champion, Larry Holmes. Spinks was ridiculed and laughed at for abandoning a division that he dominated for eight years. Spinks set out to achieve another milestone that had never been done before by a light heavyweight champion, win the heavyweight title. Larry Holmes ruled the heavyweight division for seven years and held a gaudy record of 48-0 and was on the heel of tying the immortal Rocky Marciano, who retired 49-0, the only heavyweight champion to retire undefeated. Marciano made his last title defense against the Light Heavyweight champion Archie Moore. Larry Holmes merely repeated Marciano's own history by fighting Michael Spinks. At 35, Holmes was aging but still considered a big favorite to defeat Michael Spinks and equal Marciano's record.

On this night, Spinks made history and denied Larry Holmes his chance of tying Rocky Marciano's record. Spinks was now the heavyweight champion. Having gone through a torturous training regime to transfer himself into a 200-pound fighter, Spinks outmaneuvered the champion and was able to keep Holmes from dominating with his jab. He moved in and out enough to keep the bigger man from getting inside. He did just enough to score and keep from getting hurt. Holmes, outraged at the decision and in a fit of anger, made his infamous comment that "Rocky Marciano couldn't carry my jockstrap." Larry Holmes wanted a rematch and the public wanted to see if the transformed Light Heavyweight could repeat his victory.

Holmes promised that he would get Spinks in the rematch and he almost did, coming out very hard and aggressive. He had Spinks rockin' and in trouble in the early going. Spinks survived the early Holmes onslaught and managed to stabilize the fight by the middle rounds by doing some effective boxing and keeping the aging Holmes from imposing his strength and will. It wasn't until the fourteenth round that Holmes finally caught Spinks with the biggest punch either had landed, a bone jarring straight right-hand to Spinks chin that knocked him to the other side of the ring and had him just about out. Once again, the cagey and crafty Spinks would survive to come on with a flurry in the last round to win a split decision.

Spinks' manager, Butch Lewis, decided to skip the heavyweight tournament being put together by HBO and Don Kings production. Spinks and Lewis chose a different route. After being stripped of the IBF title he won from Holmes, Spinks signed to fight the hard-hitting Gerry Cooney, who was making a comeback. After one postponement, Spinks and Cooney finally met in Atlantic City in a bout being billed as the linear heavyweight championship. Once again, the clever Spinks would survive some rough patches early in the fight and stopped Cooney in the fifth round. Two months later, the new force in the Heavyweight division, Mike Tyson won the HBO tournament by decisioning Tony Tucker. This set the stage for the fight that would settle the question, who was the real champion. Mike Tyson was at his peak and Spinks was showing signs of being on the wrong side of the hill. The public (fans) demanded these two undefeated heavyweights fight. After months of hype, these two fighters would fight their biggest fight.

The fight was not a contest. It was painfully obvious that Spinks didn't want to be there with a true heavyweight force in his prime. Within two minutes, Tyson did two things that were never before accomplished. He put Spinks down and stopped him. At almost 32, Spinks retired and never fought again. Spinks turned down many lucrative offers in the coming years to fight Evander Holyfield, when Holyfield was the undisputed champion.

It is the opinion of this writer that Tyson's defeat caused many so-called boxing experts to overlook and under appreciate the unparalleled career of Michael Spinks. When evaluating his career, it becomes quite clear that he could do it all. He could box, use the ring while utilizing his jab and reach. He could punch with either hand having the ability to score knockouts with the hook or uppercut and the right being the Spinks' jinx was almost like instant death. He thoroughly dominated a stacked Light Heavyweight division not devoid of talent like today's Light Heavyweight division. He never suffered a defeat at Light Heavyweight, something no other Light Heavyweight can claim including legends Bob Foster and Archie Moore and today's current champion, Roy Jones, Jr. He moved up to heavyweight and captured the Championship, something that all of his peers failed to do, and Roy Jones, Jr. won't try. Spinks' career is overlooked because of the Tyson defeat. History looks fondly on Billy Conn, who was knocked out by Joe Louis in a failed attempt for the heavyweight title. Archie Moore failed against Rocky Marciano, and Joe Frazier destroyed Bob Foster just as Spinks was by Tyson. Conn, Moore and Foster never achieved what Spinks did at Light Heavyweight—win the heavyweight championship. Spinks did not meet his match until three years into his career as a heavyweight. If he was fighting today, he would have a picnic in the Light Heavyweight division, Jones included. Outside of maybe three or four heavyweights, he would have his way in the Heavyweight division. Yes, Michael Spinks is one of the most under appreciated champions in history.

Holyfield: Last Stop in Atlantic City?

Holyfield: The Last Crusade Part One

By Tom Donelson

Editors note: This is the first of two pieces dealing with the Holyfield-Rahman fight. At the age of 39, Holyfield wanted one more shot at the title and this was his last crusade. The first article was my impression before the fight and the second is the actual fight and the aftermath.

On June 1st, Evander Holyfield goes into the ring to fight Hasim Rahman. For the loser, there will no longer be any chance at championship glory. The winner will still claim contender status for the Heavyweight championship, even though this may be a mirage. Holyfield has been the dominant heavyweight of the 90's, fighting every major contender and beating most. From the time he took the title from Buster Douglas to his recent trilogy with John Ruiz, Holyfield was part of the Heavyweight elite. Now, age has caught up with Holyfield, as he no longer has the quick hands or the ability to fight every minute of every round. His trilogy with Ruiz demonstrated Holyfield's erosion of skills.

There was a time when Holyfield would throw punches in bunches for every second of every round. He was the best-conditioned heavyweight and his training method enhanced his endurance. His training method allowed him to move from the cruiserweight to heavyweight division and become champion. His conditioning allowed him to survive George Foreman's onslaught and upset Riddick Bowe in their second fight. At the age of 34, Holyfield still had the endurance and strength to dominate Mike Tyson when all the experts said otherwise before the fight. By the Lewis fight, Holyfield's skills were past. As Emmanuel Steward commented after their first fight, Holyfield looked old and aged before our eyes. He could no longer impose his will and Lewis easily won the fight in the ring. The only thing that saved Holyfield's title was the judges, who ruled the fight a draw. In the second fight, Holyfied fought better but in the end, Lewis was still the better fighter. The Ruiz trilogy simply demonstrated the obvious. Holyfield was no longer a championship fighter as he only managed to split his series with a fighter who he would have knocked out just three or four years earlier.

Holyfield's pride is what keeps him fighting. As he repeatedly states, he will only quit when he is beaten badly. His fate will be similar to other great fighters such as Ali and Louis. Ali's last two fights were a lesson in humiliation, and Joe Louis' last fight resulted in his own defeat at Rocky Marciano's hand. It is every great fighter's belief that he will win every fight thus driving his success and ultimately sealing his doom. No matter how much skill they lose, they always feel that those skills will come back the next fight. The competitive spirit never dies but it forces the fighter to "cash checks" that his body can never deliver.

Holyfield has nothing left but his indomitable spirit and will. At 39, this will not be enough to capture one more championship. Will and indomitable spirit can not overcome the erosion of skills due to age. Age is the ultimate champion and no fighter is immune.

A good boxer, Rahman had one lucky punch and he became heavyweight champion when he upset Lewis in South Africa. Lewis recaptured his championship with a four round thrashing of Rahman. Rahman has a vulnerable chin and has seen the canvas floor three times in his career. The advantage that Rahman has is age as he is a decade younger than Holyfield. His mobility will give the older Holyfield fits and he has enough power to keep Holyfield off. A decade ago Holyfield would easily win this fight, but now he will enter the ring as the underdog.

I have always admired Holyfield as a fighter. He took on all challengers and never came into a fight unprepared. He was a smart fighter and when he lost to an opponent, he found a way to win a rematch. He studied his opponents and would find any weakness in his opponent's armor. Holyfield did not have the one punch knock out like a Mike Tyson but he had sufficient power to hurt his opponents. The real secret of Holyfield's success was his conditioning and this allowed him to survive tough fights including his wars with Foreman, Bowe and Tyson.

Now Holyfield is just a shell. He looks in shape and his body is still sculptured but when the bell rings, the old Holyfield will not show up. What will show is an old man, who throws one punch at a time. In the Ruiz fight, Holyfield failed to deliver effective and crisp punches. The combinations are no longer there. Holyfield's only chance is to simply impose his will and hope the younger fighter makes a mistake.

Holyfield Wins to Fight Another Day

By Tom Donelson

Editor's note: Holyfield cheated the gods to squeak out a technical victory. An accidental headbutt stopped the fight as Rahman's face sported a swelling the size of a baseball above his left eye. Holyfield had a slight lead and was declared the winner.

Holyfield managed to cheat age once again as he beat Rahman with a technical knockout. There were moments that the old Holyfield showed up as he ripped left hooks into Rahman's body but unfortunately, Holyfield could only fight in spurts. George Foreman quickly noted, "Holyfield gets tired after throwing three to five punches" but Rahman could not take advantage of the older Holyfield's spurts of inactivity.

Rahman's strength was age and an excellent jab but by the third round, Rahman was content to fight on the inside with Holyfield. This strategy sealed Rahman's fate as he fought on Holyfield's turf. Holyfield proved to be the better inside fighter as he neutralized Rahman's strength and forced a brawl. With both fighters exchanging body punches, Rahman became vulnerable to accidental headbutts. Which is what happened in the seventh round when Holyfield's head bounced right into the left side of Rahman's face and a huge swelling occurred.

Holyfield came out in the eighth round and took command during the early minutes of the round. Bothered by the baseball size swelling over his left eye, Rahman offered very little resistance. Midway through the round, the official took Rahman to the ring physician. When Rahman admitted that he could not see all of Holyfield's punches, the fight was declared over—leaving the decision in the hands of the judges.

While two of the judges had Holyfield winning all but one round, I had the fight closer. (Even though Holyfield still won.) In the fourth and fifth round, Rahman's youth took hold as he hit Holyfield with several rights followed by sharp jabbing. In the sixth round, Holyfield continued his body attacks as he continued to rip left hooks to Rahman's body. Rahman quit boxing and stood toe to toe with his older opponent. Holyfield started to control the fight but the fight had a dissatisfying ending. Holyfield's future was not satisfactorily answered as we do not know how much Holyfield had left for the later rounds. The smarts were still there though as Holyfield forced the younger fighter to fight his fight.

Holyfield only fights in spurts and his quickness is missing. What is still there is Holyfield's heart. He still has the will to win and is still capable of mustering his body to fight competitively and win over second tier challengers. While Holyfield wants one more chance at a championship, this seems so far away. His victory over Rahman is tainted by the way it ended. Rahman is a good fighter but not a great fighter and now, he is slipping out of the heavyweight contender status. Rahman is no longer a serious threat to the heavyweight belt as he moves into opponent ranking. This means that every young fighter will challenge Rahman, looking for a name fighter to put on his mantle. Holyfield can still claim that by defeating a former champion, he is still a contender. This is merely illusion, as the skills needed to win the belt one more time are no longer there. Holyfield is merely moving toward a different destiny that greets all great fighters, an ending defeat and closure to his career. As long as Holyfield can fight competitively, he will. After all, he is a fighter. It is all that he has, so the journey continues—waiting for the end to be written.

The Rumble on The River: Lewis and Tyson Fights for History

Lewis final big moment, Part One

By Tom Donelson

Editor's note: Both Tom Donelson and Frank Lotierzo gave their impression of the Lewis-Tyson Fight. They discuss their thoughts before the fight and the aftermath.

Lennox Lewis has spent the last decade, looking for respect. A massive physical specimen, Lewis combines height, power and a maneuverability that is rare in an heavyweight. Since he first won his share of the title, Lewis has been one of those heavyweights that very few boxing writers perceive as great. The reasons are many. The first is that Lewis has a tendency of losing to fighters that he has no business losing to. When he was knocked out by Oliver McCall in two rounds, most boxing experts wondered out loud, "how does a fighter as good as Lewis lose to fighter, who is nothing more than a sparring partner than a heavyweight champion." When Lewis had his chance for revenge, even this was bittersweet. Oliver McCall had a mental breakdown in the ring, refusing to defend himself and breaking out in tears-causing his disqualification. Lewis won but it was hardly a masterpiece.

Even Controversy marked his two fights over Holyfield. His first fight with Holyfield resulted in a draw despite the fact that Lewis easily outboxed Holyfield. His second fight was closer but he managed to eke out a victory. Most observers perceive this as a fight in which Lewis defeated an old Holyfield. Lewis never received his full credit for fighting and beating the best heavyweight in the 90's.

Lennox Lewis marches into his June 8th fight with Mike Tyson with one thing on his mind, to solidify his place in boxing history. His defeat at the hand of Hasim Rahman and his subsequent defeat of Rahman in the rematch merely reinforces the image of Lewis as a fighter, who is less than great. Rahman came into their first fight as an underdog and yet knocked Lewis out in the fifth round. In their second fight, Lewis dominated the fight from the opening bell and returned the favor by knocking out Rahman in the fourth round. Mike Tyson is Lewis' chance to put his stamp on boxing history.

Mike Tyson is not the fighter that he was in the late 80's. In those early days of his championship reign, he was considered unbeatable. With quick hands and knockout power, he perfected the Cus D' Amato peek-a-boo style. He ducked and weaved as he moved forward, throwing combinations in quick succession. The bloom came off Tyson's reputation when he lost to Buster Douglas and spent time in jail for rape. After his prison term, Tyson was not the same and when Holyfield dominated Tyson in their first fight and Tyson disqualified himself by trying to bite Holyfield's ear off in their second fight—Tyson's fierce reputation was no longer.

Tyson today throws one punch at a time and is easier to hit. He can still knock anyone out with his power and Tyson has only lost to two fighters, Holyfield and Douglas. This upcoming fight is intriguing since there are several questions, mostly revolving around Lewis. Lewis' tendency to be careless in key moments and his suspect chin makes a Tyson victory a real possibility.

At this point in either fighter's career, Lewis is the better fighter. Lewis can easily dominate this fight with his superior reach and punishing left jab. Somewhere in this fight, Tyson will hit Lewis and the big question is whether Lewis can stand the power of Tyson. Lewis's left jab will drill Tyson and Tyson's has shown that he can be beaten by a boxer-punchers such as Holyfield and Douglas.

For Tyson, this fight is redemption. As a man who has been trained in boxing folklore by Cus D' Amato and Jimmy Jacobs, Tyson always viewed himself as one of boxing's great. The last several years have diminished Tyson's reputation but this victory over Lewis will establish Tyson as a great fighter, at least in Tyson's mind. It is easily argued that neither fighter will rank among the greatest but this fight still pits two of the most successful heavyweight fighters over the past fifteen years. This fight has it's own drama and appeal, and this fight has been in the planning ever since Lewis defeated Holyfield in their second fight.

Lewis has the style to beat Tyson. He can box and with his superior reach, should dominate Tyson from the outside. Just like the Tua fight, Lewis will jab and look for his opening. Tyson's only chance is to put on the pressure from the opening bell and attack since Lewis' vulnerability is his chin, especially in the early rounds.

Lewis irritates boxing purists since he never fights to please the crowd but to win. When he fought Holyfield and Tua, he remained satisfied to box from the outside and not to mix it up. Lewis never allowed his opponents a chance to punish him. Boxing fans may not appreciate Lewis' style of fighting from the outside and tying up his opponent—though it does produce wins. Lewis never allows his ego to get in the way of his strategy. Another thing is that Lewis has a mind and can put sentences together. What boxing fan can really like a fighter whose hobbies include playing chess? It is hardly the hobby that speaks of masculinity. Before Lewis' last fight, Rahman challenged the single Lewis on his sexual orientation. (Some boxing fans view a chess playing fighter who is single as possibly gay and Rahman insinuated that Lewis was homosexual. Lewis answered Rahman's accusation with a fourth round shellacking.)

On June 8th, Lennox Lewis has one big opportunity to answer all the questions about his boxing skills. Defeating Tyson, Lewis at the age of 36 can finally win the one big fight that has eluded him. He should win. In boxing, having superior boxing skills does not always translate into victory. Throughout Lewis's career, boxing fans and experts found

Lewis to be an enigma and they are looking for answers to the riddle that is Lewis. After June 8th, Lewis will no longer be a mystery.

Tyson: Final moment of glory?

By Frank Lotierzo

Editor's note: These are Frank Lotierzo's observations before Tyson and Lewis. Frank's belief was that Tyson would find a way to defeat Lewis.

It is Tuesday, June 4th, 2002 and I know that many of my friends in the boxing world are picking Lewis. On Saturday, June 8th, Tyson will knock out Lewis. Then the fun begins; every moron will want to make Tyson, history's greatest heavyweight champion. Talk about spin; wait till you hear this crap. Yea, when Mike's back was against it, he beat the man that Holyfield could not. Just wait until he gets his hands on Holyfield a third time. The Tyson lovers will declare Tyson the greatest of this era. I thought Holyfield ended the Tyson mythology, but Tyson is here to haunt me. I've dreaded this since Lewis beat Holyfield. Deep down, I 've always had this voice in the back of my head, saying, "Frank, you better hope that Lennox Lewis is not the fighter standing between Tyson and Immortality." Guess who is standing between Tyson and immortality? I have dreaded June 8th for about three years. And now it is about to happen.

You have to know what is going to happen for no other reason that I do not want it to happen. I never wanted one fighter to beat another fighter so badly in my life. And this is the biggest reason why it won't happen. Lewis is the guy standing between Tyson and Immortality, a guy with no chin, who either fights scare or not to lose. If I had managed Tyson and looked for the fighter to redeem his place in history, Lewis is the guy I would order. Yeah, a guy who goes with one shot by guys who do not have reputation for being punchers, a guy who fight scared and a guy who fights most of the time not to get knocked out.

After seeing Rahman versus Holyfield, and knowing that Lewis' legend is based on beating Rahman in the rematch—Tyson will end Lewis' career. I feel like I am on death row waiting for Saturday around midnight. Lewis will not be able to tie up Tyson as some think.

Lewis may be too tall for Tyson. If Tyson moves his head and is not stationary, it will be difficult for Lewis to grab and tie him up. Lewis may find Tyson hard to find with his jab, if Tyson gets low as Frazier did with Ali. Lewis is going to be bothered by punching down. Tua did not do this in his fight with Lewis and Tyson can nullify his jab if he does this. This is a fight that Lewis cannot win. If he knocks Tyson out, all of the Tyson apologists will say, he did not beat the best Tyson. If Tyson knocks Lewis out, then Lewis is a bum. Whoever is the winner, will be regarded the better fighter.

As I stated, the X factor is the Lewis chin. If Lewis had Holyfield's chin, we would be asking if Tyson could take the Lewis right for 12 rounds.

I have said since 1986, Tyson is the most overrated Heavyweight champion of all-time. Right now, he is little underrated after his fight with Nielson and Lewis is slightly overrated coming off his fight with Rahman. Say what you want about Tyson, he is a force because he can really punch and get his punches off quickly. He still can do both, if he is in shape. Besides, I am terrible at picking Lewis' fights. When I felt he would win, he either lost or struggled. Tyson in Two. I hope I am wrong.

Why Tyson Lost
By Frank Lotierzo

Editor's note: Frank briefly dissects Tyson's performance in his last big moment.

Why did Tyson lose?
*He's not good enough, never was!

*Notice that he had movement in the first minute or two in the first round.

I've always said that once Tyson gets hit, he stops. He stops throwing combinations and stops moving his head. When he fought Buster Douglas, he threw half as many punches per round as he did in previous fights. The reason? Because Buster Douglas was hitting him with jabs and caused Tyson to stop throwing combinations—forcing him to throw one punch at a time. Lewis did the same thing and that is why Tyson lost.

In the end, his makeup inside is the difference between Tyson and the Great fighters before him. When he stated that he needed a couple of fights that should have told me that Tyson knew his own fate. Now he will have those two or three fights but he may never get another chance at a title.

Lewis' Finest Moment

By Tom Donelson

Editor's note: This is the post fight analysis of Lewis' victory over Tyson. And now the debate begins, what is Lewis' place in boxing history.

Lennox Lewis' finest moment finally happened on June 8th. From the second round on, Lewis showed his boxing superiority as he gave a boxing lesson to Mike Tyson. After this fight, Lewis' could lay claim to being the best of the past decade. Only Holyfield's accomplishments can be compared to Lewis' and this fight established Lewis' legacy as a top ten all time heavyweight.

From the opening bell, tension was high as both fighters met in the center of the ring. Lewis connected on two uppercuts, but these were Lewis' only effective punches of the round as he spent most of the round holding Tyson. Tyson, trying to recapture the Tyson of old, bobbed and weaved to set up his power punches. He jabbed to get inside of Lewis but as he approached Lewis, Lewis grabbed the smaller Tyson and borrowing a page from Ali, pushed Tyson's neck down.

This helped wear Tyson down and, while Tyson won the round it would be his last hurrah. He would not capture another round in the fight.

The second round, Lewis dominated. Jabbing and moving, Lewis scored heavily as Tyson no longer bobbed and weaved. No longer capable of throwing a large volume of punches and now throwing one punch at a time, Tyson looked all of his 35 years of age. He started to fight standing up and Lewis' jab found its target consistently. Tyson blocked Lewis' feared right with his head, hardly the strategy that wins fights against Lewis.

The fourth round showed what was evident; Lewis was the better fighter. At the end of the round a Lewis right nailed Tyson. As Tyson started to fall down, Lewis aided Tyson's fall by pushing him down, and added a punch to the back for good measure. For that, Lewis lost a point by deduction, but it did not matter. Tyson was finished. With both eyes cut and swelling, Tyson was losing his vision and no longer was picking up Lewis' right. As Tyson's corner exhorted their warrior to throw punches in bunches; Emmanuel Steward was getting into Lewis' face. Steward yelled to Lewis after the fifth round, "get the mother fucker out, he is ready to go" as he sent his fighter out to the center of the ring. Lewis continued to hit Tyson with combinations and Tyson no longer responded.

As Lewis' gets back to his corner, Steward yelled once again, "finish the SOB, he is ready to go, don't mess around with this guy." As Steward was getting into his fighter's face, Tyson's corner begged their fighter to just throw punches. Tyson's trainer, Ronnie Shields told Tyson, "I will not allow you to get a beating"—telling Tyson, in effect, he will stop the fight if Tyson does not show more in the next round.

The fateful eighth round ended Tyson's quest for a championship. As Tyson's face met a Lewis right, Tyson hit the canvas for an eight count. Tyson began one last counter attack. Near the end of the round, Tyson threw one big haymaker—a vicious right cross. The punch hit nothing but air. Lewis countered with a classic right cross that hit Tyson in the sweet spot and Tyson went down for good.

By beating Tyson, even an old Tyson, Lewis has now beaten two of the best fighters over the past 15 years. His place in boxing history is now secure. For Tyson, this ends his career as a serious championship contender. Tyson's own behavior after the fight showed a docile Tyson. No bravado, no weird declaration about eating Lewis' children or putting his fist through Lewis' skull—Tyson merely accepted his fate. If nothing else, he was the perfect sportsman, begging for a rematch.

Tyson never believed he could win. After the fight, he stated that he needed a couple of tune-ups and even his call for a rematch seemed insincere. That is what Tyson is reduced to, begging for rematch so he can get one more big payday. For Tyson, fighting now means making enough money to pay for his life style. After the fight, he conceded that much of the grossness was meant to sell tickets, and I suspect that his pre-fight ranting masked the lack of confidence that Tyson had in winning the fight. If nothing else, Tyson has a durable chin since he was eating Lewis' right all night. What is missing is the speed and quickness that categorized his career at the beginning. Tyson can no longer bob and weave for an entire fight and the famous peek-a-boo style that he inherited from Cus D' Amato is but a distant memory. Throwing one punch at a time, Tyson became easy to defend against. Like Evander Holyfield, Tyson is reduced to fighting in spurts and hoping to hit a home run with his power. He can no longer fight the full three minutes of a round.

Tyson no longer has any claims of greatness. He was a good fighter but he will never make the great category. In a boxing career, one or two fights define a fighter's career. Ali's defeats of George Foreman and Joe Frazier allowed Ali to claim the greatest of all times title. Tyson lost to both Holyfield and Lewis, the two best fighters over the past decade and no longer has any claim to boxing immortality. As a young man,

Tyson was the baddest man but not now. The Tyson circus is now over. Boxing validation is based on winning the big fights.

Lennox Lewis is a different fighter. At the age of 36, Lewis shows no signs of slowing down; it is as if he has turned back the aging clock. At an age when most fighters are in decline, Lewis still has his speed and mobility. Like a fine wine, Lewis continues to get better. Lewis' fourteen championship victories are the fourth best among heavyweights and only Holyfield's accomplishment is comparable over the past 15 years. Both men beat the top heavyweights of their generation and they now join other historical figures among the Heavyweight greats. Neither Holyfield nor Lewis dominated their era like Ali or Louis, but they were the best of their era. Lewis, like Holyfied, is one of the ten best fighters since the 30's and he has the ability to adapt to any situation.

For Lewis, this fight showed the world that he is the baddest guy in the universe for the moment. For Tyson, this fight was just a payday and he no longer has the fire that once made him great. For Lewis, his future is now secure and he has nothing left to prove. Lewis' finest moment has now come, and he has beaten a renowned fighter. Lewis is no longer a mystery and at the age of 36, he now gets his due.

Final Thoughts on Holyfield and Lewis

By Tom Donelson

It takes a number of years to determine a fighter's place in boxing history, and certainly we will need years to measure Lennox Lewis and Evander Holyfield. What we do know is that for the past 15 years, Evander Holyfield and Lennox Lewis defeated the best fighters of their era. There is no dispute that both fighters can easily be ranked in the top ten of best heavyweights since the 30's. The only thing that time will tell is where they rank among the greatest.

Evander Holyfield had the warrior mentality, regardless of the opponent—he took no quarter nor did he give any. Lennox Lewis depended upon guile, mobility and his power to win. Holyfield built himself up from a cruiserweight to heavyweight status and had the heart to compete with bigger fighters. Lewis was one of those big men that Holyfield competed against, but he had superior boxing ability. Despite his height and weight, he could move and jab with ease. If Lewis had one fault, it was a questionable chin that was demonstrated on two occasions—against Oliver McCall and Hasim Rahman. Holyfield, on the other hand, had one of the most durable chins and was stopped only once, in his third fight with Riddock Bowe.

Holyfield had more wars and tougher fights. His bouts with Bowe, Foreman, Mercer, Tyson, and Lewis took their toll on the smaller Holyfield. Lewis was spared a bout with Bowe, who chose not to fight him. He did not get the opportunity to fight Foreman but did fight Holyfield two times, besting him once officially and fighting to a controversial draw in their first match. The Holyfield that Lewis fought was past his prime and no longer the great fighter that engaged in those previous wars, and yet, both fighters went the distance. Lewis fought what was in front of him and when he finished off Tyson, he secured his own legacy alongside Holyfield. Lewis and Holyfield proved to be the best warriors of this generation. In the end, they will march into history as two of boxing's best along with Foreman, Frazier, Holmes, and Marciano.

Tyson, No Longer

By Tom Donelson

When Mike Tyson destroyed Michael Spinks, it would be his highwater point in his career. At the age of 22, Mike Tyson was the king of his world—the baddest man in the universe. When Tyson walked into the ring, his opponent concluded, "resistance was futile." Tyson was to be Cus D' Amato's last big project in boxing, the perfect fighting machine. With quick cat like reflexes and capable of knocking out an opponent with either hand, Tyson merely mowed his opponent down. Tyson was the youngest fighter to win a title and within two years, he would be youngest to lose his title.

Tyson resembles a Greek tragedy, trained to be invincible and the greatest of all times—Tyson fell victim to the larceny of others and his own hubris. When Tyson hit the ground from a Buster Douglas' uppercut, the mantle of invincibility was gone. After two prison terms and two defeats at the hand of Holyfield, Lewis was Tyson's last chance to salvage his career and place in boxing history. When Tyson was a young fighter, Cus D' Amato and his friend, Jimmy Jacobs showed Tyson their catalog of fight films. He understood very clearly what it took to get to the top and stay there. After the death of Jacobs, Tyson lost his bearing and his career would turn for the worse with personal problems dealing Tyson blows to his boxing career.

Lewis finally demolished the myth that was Tyson, and as Tyson fell to the ground, we could imagine what could have been. Tyson had the tools to be one of the greatest but he lost his discipline to maintain his title. At the beginning of his career, he merely went out and won. No theatrics, no threats or gross behavior, Tyson acted the perfect gentleman after a victory. When the 90's came around and Tyson no longer was king—the theatrics began. He would bite ears, try to break boxers' arms, hit after the bell and make obscene gestures at press conferences. No longer depending upon his own skills to win fights, the circus began.

Like Louis in his last days, Tyson fights for money and not for the joy of the sports. Compared to Holyfield, who actually likes to fight; Tyson appears burned out. When Joe Louis came back from his retirement to fight to pay off IRS bills, the fire was extinguished. No longer the Louis of old, Joe Louis lost to Ezzard Charles and Rocky Marciano. The fighter, shorn of his skills, merely crumbled in the ring. Tyson is exactly the same position as Louis, no longer capable of beating the best in the division. Tyson is still a good fighter, capable of beating most fighters, he just can not beat the best in the division. As his skills continue to deteriorate, the hyenas that benefited financially from his rise will do so as he slips down to oblivion and retirement. Like the characters from the 1950's movie, "The Harder They Fall", Tyson will be part of a new circus, the decline of the once great fighter as his handlers will handle his decline as they handled his rise. They will make money off the carcass that once was Tyson. Tyson may yet resemble the Anthony Quinn character in "Requiem for a Heavyweight" as he joins the WWF to make extra money.

Tyson could have been great but his handlers mismanaged his career and betrayed him. Tyson, former champion, has reached the end of the road as title contender. Now he will be an opponent over whom others leap frog to their title shot, provided they beat Tyson. Tyson's destiny was to be the greatest, but in the end—his skills became overshadowed by Holyfield and Lewis. Tyson may end up a footnote, just another pug that held the title, with nothing special for it. Boxing historians will not be kind to Tyson and that will be the unkindest cut of all. To be ignored, or worse, to be mocked. For Tyson, the circus has ended.

Tommy "The Duke" Morrison: Golden Boy Turns to Dust.

By Tom Donelson

In the early 90's, Tommy "The Duke" Morrison began his march toward the Heavyweight pot of gold. A good-looking gentleman with the right skin pigmentation, Morrison had the potential of being a marketing golden calf. He began his career by beating the usual suspects of stiffs. Then he began the second part of his career, beating up on old fighters with a name on their way down. His fight with Jimmy "Quick" Tillis, who went the distance with Mike Tyson, was supposed to be his first test against a wily veteran. Early in Tillis career, he had quick hands and feet to pound an opponent and escape from danger. What Tillis lacked was a Heavyweight punch. The crafty veteran, alleged as very able to teach an up and comer a thing or two, was at the end of his career. Against "The Duke", "Quick's" age slowed his reflexes. He was out "quick" in the first round.

While many point to Tillis as another stiff on Morrison's record, I remember a line used by George Foreman. Asked if a recent opponent, ranked tenth in the world, was good, Foreman replied, "I hope not." The point? Good Boxers are supposed to end fights quickly. If they end them too quickly, then the opponents are bums. If the opponent stays around, then the slugger is overrated. The one thing that Morrison had was a punch and knew when to end the fight-good timing.

Pinklon Thomas, a former heavyweight champion, was supposed to be a tougher match. Thomas, a 33-year-old former heavyweight champion, had power in both hands along with a good left jab. Against Morrison, his reflexes were slow and his jab failed to connect. I could only count one jab that actually landed. The Thomas defense consisted of blocking "The Duke's" blow with his head. After one round and a nasty cut over Thomas' eyes, the fight was over.

This fight merely signaled that Thomas' career was soon to be over and it proved that Morrison had knock out power. Before this fight, Pinklon Thomas managed to last 9 rounds against Bowe, who was to become the heavyweight champion by upsetting Holyfield.

At this point in Morrison's career, he passed all the initial tests but was yet to be truly tested by a giant. Then came his battle against Ray Mercer. Mercer was one of those fighters with concrete in his head. You could hit the man with a 2 by 4 and he would still be standing. Tommy "The Duke" Morrison challenged Mercer for the WBO title, which was a minor title but a title, nonetheless. This was the fight that would propel Morrison to the big time.

The first three rounds, Morrison dominated the action, backing Mercer up. Morrison hit Mercer with every possible combination and from every angle. Up and down, combination after combination raining upon Mercer, but Mercer remained standing. At the end of the fourth round, Mercer hit Morrison with a vicious right hand that sent the young challenger reeling into the rope. Morrison staggered to his corner as the bell rang, ending the round. I immediately turned to a friend and told him that Morrison was finished. After dominating for three and half rounds, Morrison had nothing left and demonstrated his greatest flaw—a glass chin. As the fifth round opened, Mercer pounded Morrison into the rope and threw about 18 unanswered punches as Morrison sat helpless against the rope. In one of the most vicious knockouts I have ever witnessed,—Morrison's eyes rolled back as he slipped to the canvas from the rope that was previously holding him up. He was carried out of the ring.

After this devastating defeat, Morrison went back to the drawing board. He worked his way back to a fight with George Foreman and here, Morrison demonstrated that he could execute a plan B. Normally a straight head slugger, Morrison's corner realized against Foreman this would be suicide. Morrison's weak chin would not survive Foreman's onslaught; so Morrison executed Plan B—he became a boxer. Using his quicker hands, he jabbed and moved away from Foreman's power. Foreman, shocked at this development, spent the entire fight chasing his younger opponent and losing the WBO title.

Morrison decided to defend his title against Michael Bennett and here the vulnerable chin became exposed once again. Morrison charged his opponent and ran right into a left hook. Down went Morrison. "The Duke" struggled to get up, only to hit the canvas again. Morrison would go down one more time before the fight was stopped. Morrison, once again, was forced into the depth of boxing's rankings forced to work his way up again. Being an attractive white fighter enhanced his value and he was never far from the Heavyweight crown. He even starred in a "Rocky" movie with Sylvester Stallone, to show that he had movie charisma.

While Morrison enjoyed the trappings of being a heavyweight contender, he lacked the heart to make it to the top. After the Foreman fight, he never improved and often partied at night. When he faced Lennox Lewis, Morrison's abilities slipped. He lasted six rounds, but found himself on the floor four times before the referee ended the fight, counting "The Duke" out. His career was effectively over, but worse news was still to come. Preparing for a fight, a routine blood test showed the HIV virus and Morrison's party past came back to haunt him. He never fought again.

Morrison is a tale that is often told in sports, a young talent who never fulfills his potential. Morrison was blessed with a wicked left hook and powerful right hand but he was also cursed with a vulnerable chin and a lethargic attitude toward training. Whether it was the lack of dedication or his chin that doomed his career is hard to say. What can be said, Tommy "The Duke" Morrison had the chance to be a champion. As Marlon Brando's character remarked in the movie, "On the Waterfront", "I coulda been a contender." Potential is a valuable asset to waste.

Fres Oquendo: Going for the Top

By Tom Donelson

(Written before the Oquendo-David Izon fight, but you can replace Obed Sullivan with Izon and the article can stay the same including the small matter of Izon losing his fight to Oquendo.)

Fres Oquendo was one of those up and coming heavyweight fighters, undefeated and ready to break into the top 10, when he faced Obed Sullivan for Sullivan's NABF championship belt. For Oquendo, the NABF championship was a stepping stone to bigger fights and a chance for a world heavyweight championship. For Sullivan, keeping his minor championship belt meant maybe one more big payday. Oquendo, trained by Tito Trinidad's father, came out smoking and rocked Obed with several bombs. After this impressive first round, he changed course and was content with moving and flicking his powerful jab into Obed's face. Obed looked liked the aged fighter that he was, feeling the effect of every punch. Swollen and cut, Obed knew the score. There was no tomorrow for him, and every round he kept moving forward, only to absorb more punishment. Like the Anthony Quinn character in "Requiem for a Heavyweight", he pressed the action and prepared to go out on his shield. Sullivan was fighting a younger and quicker fighter and nothing he did worked. Oquendo was in total control and by the 10th round, Sullivan's legs no longer could hold the old warrior up. He was rocked with several shots and barely made it back to the corner. The 11th round saw the end of Obed Sullivan's career as a top ten fighter as Oquendo sent the proud warrior down for the count. Blood spurting out of his nose and his loved ones looking on in horror, Sullivan lay dazed and unaware of his location. Helped out of the ring, Sullivan lost his NABF title belt and slowly receded into boxing's purgatory of warm up fights in places like Des Moines.

For most fighters, Sullivan's fate is their fate. A fighter begins the spring of his career full of promise and hope. Oquendo is now in the spring of his career, undefeated and the world before him. The moment of truth comes when a young fighter fights the elite with this moment of truth dividing the pretenders and serious contenders. When Sullivan moved up in competition early in his career, he lost. David Tua knocked Sullivan out in one round in 1997 and that effectively ended Sullivan's chances of heavyweight glory. Now with this recent defeat, Sullivan faces the prospect of being nothing more than a trial horse for young guns to beat up on. For a fighter like Sullivan, there will be no more big pay dates. Occasional TV slots on Fox or ESPN2 and a life of warm-up fights; Sullivan now faces the real question of a fighter. Do I keep fighting and taking punishment when the return on investment is no longer there? This is the toughest part of any fighter's career, deciding when to hang up the gloves and get on with his life.

As for Fres Oquendo, he is a potential star but we will never know how good he is until he faces the best of the heavyweights. A good athlete with a great team behind him, he has developed from a raw talent to a legitimate heavyweight challenger. Only the future will determine his fate. He could be one of the elite's of the Heavyweight division or he could be a mere opponent. We will know soon how quickly Oquendo's fate is similar to Sullivan.

(After his fight with Izon, Oquendo fought David Tua. After easily dominating the fight for the first eight rounds, Oquendo makes one mistake and the hard-hitting Tua knocked out the young Puerto Rican, handing Oquendo his first loss. Now we will see whether Oquendo learned from his mistake or if he becomes an opponent like Izon and Sullivan.)

Sugar Ray Robinson: The Perfect Boxer

By Tom Donelson

When you look in a dictionary for the definition of boxing, a picture of Sugar Ray Robinson will appear. Sugar Ray could do it all. He could box and he could knock out an opponent with just one punch. His ability to take a punch allowed him to survive without ever being knocked out or stopped-at least by human hands. The only time Sugar Ray Robinson was ever stopped, it was by Mother Nature. Sugar Ray Robinson, easily winning the light heavy weight fight against Joey Maxim, fell victim to extreme heat when he could not answer the bell for the 14th round. Heat prostration ended Robinson's shot at the light heavyweight championship.

Born Walker Smith, Jr. in the motor city of Detroit, Sugar Ray had an outstanding amateur career winning 85 bouts including 69 knock-outs. Forty of these knockouts were in the first round! His professional debut was no less spectacular as he won his first 40 fights in a row before suffering his first loss to the tough Jake LaMotta. He revenged that loss three weeks later.

On December 20, 1946, he won his first title taking the welter-weight championship from Tommy Bell. He went on to dominate the welterweight division. The one fight that would change Robinson was his confrontation with Jimmy Doyle. Before the fight, Robinson had a premonition that tragedy would strike and it did. As Robinson recalled, "I dreamed that I knocked him out and he died right in the ring. I called the commission and everybody and I said I'm not fight-ing." After being ensured that it was just a dream, Sugar Ray Robinson marched into the ring and fulfilled the tragedy predicated in his dream. Jimmy Doyle did not leave the ring alive.

For Sugar Ray, this fight would change the way he approached the fight game. As he stated, "I didn't want to fight, because I did not like violence. And for a long time after that I could only fight just hard enough to win. I didn't want to hit that punch, that KO punch." Sugar could make such a strategy work, as he did not need to knock out opponents to win. He could dance his way to victory, a virtuoso of the ring with superior speed and foot movement. After dominating the welterweight, he challenged Jake LaMotta for LaMotta's Middleweight championship belt. This was the last of six fights these two warriors fought. Jake LaMotta had a concrete head, and a heart that stated, "you had to kill me to beat me." LaMotta's toughness and awkward style countered Sugar Ray's boxing style. The fight alternated between a street fight and occasional boxing gem. Sugar Ray's movement and ability to take a punch allowed him to ward off the charging LaMotta. The 10th round was LaMotta's last chance to win as he blew all caution to the wind and went for the knockout. After Robinson survived the 10th, he went on to easily win the 11th and 12th rounds. The 13th round, long memorialized in the movie, "Raging Bull" proved the character of both men.

Robinson struck LaMotta with combination after combination. LaMotta stood by the rope, with eyes shut due to the force of Robinson's punches. But LaMotta's will power kept him standing and he even taunted Robinson, telling him,"you can not knock me out, Sugar Ray." LaMotta would not go easily and would not take a knee. The referee finally halted the proceeding with LaMotta holding on to the rope in an effort to keep standing. As Robinson admitted years later, "you hit this guy with everything and he'd just act like you're crazy."

This fight demonstrated what few ever knew or suspected about Robinson, he could take a punch from a heavy-handed puncher. Robinson took a vacation touring Europe. He didn't train properly and thus lost his belt to the British Randy Turpin in an upset. He would regain his title back with a 10th round knockout. The later fight was typical Robinson. With his eyes cut and profuse bleeding threatening his title chances, Robinson went into the 10th round needing a knockout. With a barrage of accurate punches finding their target, Robinson ended the affair.

Robinson challenged Joey Maxim for the Light Heavyweight on a sweltering summer night. The heat took its toll, as the chief referee had to quit and be replaced in the 10th round. Robinson was easily winning the fight but the heat was taking its toll. Robinson dreamed the night before that he died in the fight. As the 13th round ended, Robinson could no longer fight. Heat prostration set in, and as Robinson recalled, "I was incoherent all night from that heat prostration. I passed out. But I went longer than the referee." Joey Maxim defended his title with Mother Nature aiding his cause.

Robinson tiring of the fight game, retired to pursue a show business career. After two years layoff and boredom setting in, Robinson went back into the ring. He won the title back from Bobo Olson with a second round knockout. Past 35 years old and having won the Middleweight title for the third time, Robinson was in the twilight of his career—but there were still great moments left in his career.

Gene Fullmer dominated the older Robinson, even knocking Robinson down in the 7th round. Youth and aggressive fighting style took its toll on Robinson and Fullmer took a 15 round decision to claim Robinson's title. In the rematch, Robinson knocked Fullmer out with a picture perfect left hook in the 5th round after splitting the first four rounds. Robinson would lose the title again to the rugged Carmen Basilio. Carmen Basilio, who felt that Robinson dissed him years before, fought a non-stop aggressive fight that forced the older Robinson to back up most of the fight and took the decision. Basilio's left hook constantly found the mark and Robinson fought off the rope for most of the fight. The rematch would be Robinson's last great moment. Close to 38 and beyond his prime, Robinson summoned up all his greatness for one more effort to recapture the championship. In the fifth round, Robinson nailed Basilio with a left hook that swelled up Basilio's eyes. From this point, Robinson gained the upper hand, retaking the championship with a split decision. Robinson would maintain his championship for two more years before losing it to Paul Pender. Robinson would attempt to win the title one more time with two last fights against Gene Fullmer. The first one was a draw, even though he could easily have been declared the winner. But a draw favored the champion Fullmer, with Fullmer beating the 41 year old Robinson one last time. His championship days were over.

Robinson never could escape the lure of the ring, and even after his championship form no longer existed, he kept fighting five more years. He fought a few quality fighters but mostly he fought mediocre opponents. On November 10th, 1965, Sugar Ray Robinson entered the ring for the last time. With Madison Square Garden as a background, Sugar Ray would lose a decision to Joey Archer. The magic, long since gone, could not be recaptured even for one more night. Sugar Ray's career ended the way most boxers, losing to mediocre opponents and age.

Sugar Ray's post boxing career also resembled most boxers. After a lifetime of spending extravagance and divorce settlements from his many wives, the money was gone. He appeared in a few television shows but for the most part, Robinson soon became a charity case himself. At the end, suffering the ravages of Alzheimer's disease, Robinson would die with no memory of even his own greatness.

Sugar Ray Robinson is recognized today as the greatest pound for pound fighter ever. And with good reason. There was never a fighter who combined boxing skills and the punching power that Sugar Ray Leonard could. A slick boxer, he could avoid being hit, and with power in both hands, he could end a fight in an instant. He stood as a model for other fighters such as Muhammad Ali, and inspired a whole generation of boxers. Sugar Ray was the ultimate fighting machine.

About the Authors

✦

Tom Donelson and Frank Lotierzo

"Viewing Boxing From Ringside" reviews both the history and the intricacies of Boxing. Frank Lotierzo and Tom Donelson review past historical figures of boxing as well as the journeymen and in some cases challenge some widely held beliefs. The reader will become familiar with slighted individuals such as Harry Wills, the great African-American fighter, denied a shot of the heavyweight title due to his skin color or the ambiguity of Floyd Patterson's career. Mr. Lotierzo and Mr. Donelson add perspective to the sweet science not seen and leave no sacred cows unchallenged.

Frank Lotierzo had an excellent amateur career and started his professional career undefeated before injuries cut it short. Since then, he has become boxing historian through study and reviewing fight films. His works has appeared in many boxing publications including Boxing Illustrated, K.O. magazine, Fight Game Magazine, Fightnews, Cyberboxingzone and Boxing Insider. In the past, he has co-hosted varied radio programs in the Atlantic City area and is presently host of "Toe to Toe" ESPN Radio 1490/1580 in Atlantic City, where he presently lives.

Tom Donelson has been a free lance writer on a wide variety of issues for the past two decades. His work has appeared in Kansas City Star, Cedar Rapid Gazette, Fort Wayne News—Sentinel, Fort Wayne Gazette, K.C. Jones, National Review, New York Press and Cyberboxingzone.com. Mr. Donelson has been a guest lecturer throughout the Midwest and presently resides in Marion, Iowa.

0-595-23748-7

Printed in the United States
1020000004B/163